OPPOSING
VIEWPOINTS®
SERIES

National Service

Other Books of Related Interest:

Opposing Viewpoints Series
Student Life

At Issue Series
What Is Humanity's Greatest Challenge?

Current Controversies Series
Patriotism

"Congress shall make no law ... abridging the freedom of speech, or of the press."

First Amendment to the US Constitution

The basic foundation of our democracy is the First Amendment guarantee of freedom of expression. The *Opposing Viewpoints* series is dedicated to the concept of this basic freedom and the idea that it is more important to practice it than to enshrine it.

OPPOSING VIEWPOINTS® SERIES

National Service

Louise I. Gerdes, Book Editor

GREENHAVEN PRESS
A part of Gale, Cengage Learning

GALE
CENGAGE Learning™

Detroit • New York • San Francisco • New Haven, Conn • Waterville, Maine • London

GALE
CENGAGE Learning™

Christine Nasso, *Publisher*
Elizabeth Des Chenes, *Managing Editor*

© 2011 Greenhaven Press, a part of Gale, Cengage Learning.

Gale and Greenhaven Press are registered trademarks used herein under license.

For more information, contact:
Greenhaven Press
27500 Drake Rd.
Farmington Hills, MI 48331-3535
Or you can visit our Internet site at gale.cengage.com

For product information and technology assistance, contact us at

Gale Customer Support, 1-800-877-4253
For permission to use material from this text or product, submit all requests online at www.cengage.com/permissions

Further permissions questions can be emailed to permissionrequest@cengage.com

Articles in Greenhaven Press anthologies are often edited for length to meet page require-ments. In addition, original titles of these works are changed to clearly present the main thesis and to explicitly indicate the author's opinion. Every effort is made to ensure that Greenhaven Press accurately reflects the original intent of the authors. Every effort has been made to trace the owners of copyrighted material.

Cover Image copyright © Jason Reed/Reuters/Corbis.

LIBRARY OF CONGRESS CATALOGING-IN-PUBLICATION DATA

National service / Louise I. Gerdes, book editor.
    p. cm. -- (Opposing viewpoints)
    Includes bibliographical references and index.
    ISBN 978-0-7377-5233-5 (hardcover) -- ISBN 978-0-7377-5234-2 (pbk.)
    1. Voluntarism--Government policy--United States--Juvenile literature. 2. Civic improvement--United States--Juvenile literature. 3. Community development--United States--Juvenile literature. I. Gerdes, Louise I., 1953-
    HN90.V64N36 2011
    361.6--dc22
                                                                        2010054416

Printed in the United States of America
1 2 3 4 5 6 7 15 14 13 12 11

Contents

Chapter 3: What Role Should Service Learning Play in Society?

Chapter 4: What Role Should the Government Play in National Service?

Why Consider Opposing Viewpoints?

> *"The only way in which a human being can make some approach to knowing the whole of a subject is by hearing what can be said about it by persons of every variety of opinion and studying all modes in which it can be looked at by every character of mind. No wise man ever acquired his wisdom in any mode but this."*
>
> John Stuart Mill

In our media-intensive culture it is not difficult to find differing opinions. Thousands of newspapers and magazines and dozens of radio and television talk shows resound with differing points of view. The difficulty lies in deciding which opinion to agree with and which "experts" seem the most credible. The more inundated we become with differing opinions and claims, the more essential it is to hone critical reading and thinking skills to evaluate these ideas. *Opposing Viewpoints* books address this problem directly by presenting stimulating debates that can be used to enhance and teach these skills. The varied opinions contained in each book examine many different aspects of a single issue. While examining these conveniently edited opposing views, readers can develop critical thinking skills such as the ability to compare and contrast authors' credibility, facts, argumentation styles, use of persuasive techniques, and other stylistic tools. In short, the *Opposing Viewpoints* Series is an ideal way to attain the higher-level thinking and reading skills so essential in a culture of diverse and contradictory opinions.

In addition to providing a tool for critical thinking, *Opposing Viewpoints* books challenge readers to question their own strongly held opinions and assumptions. Most people form their opinions on the basis of upbringing, peer pressure, and personal, cultural, or professional bias. By reading carefully balanced opposing views, readers must directly confront new ideas as well as the opinions of those with whom they disagree. This is not to argue simplistically that everyone who reads opposing views will—or should—change his or her opinion. Instead, the series enhances readers' understanding of their own views by encouraging confrontation with opposing ideas. Careful examination of others' views can lead to the readers' understanding of the logical inconsistencies in their own opinions, perspective on why they hold an opinion, and the consideration of the possibility that their opinion requires further evaluation.

Evaluating Other Opinions

To ensure that this type of examination occurs, *Opposing Viewpoints* books present all types of opinions. Prominent spokespeople on different sides of each issue as well as well-known professionals from many disciplines challenge the reader. An additional goal of the series is to provide a forum for other, less known, or even unpopular viewpoints. The opinion of an ordinary person who has had to make the decision to cut off life support from a terminally ill relative, for example, may be just as valuable and provide just as much insight as a medical ethicist's professional opinion. The editors have two additional purposes in including these less known views. One, the editors encourage readers to respect others' opinions—even when not enhanced by professional credibility. It is only by reading or listening to and objectively evaluating others' ideas that one can determine whether they are worthy of consideration. Two, the inclusion of such viewpoints encourages the important critical thinking skill of objectively evaluating an author's credentials and bias. This evaluation will illuminate an author's reasons for taking a particular stance on an issue and will aid in readers' evaluation of the author's ideas.

It is our hope that these books will give readers a deeper understanding of the issues debated and an appreciation of the complexity of even seemingly simple issues when good and honest people disagree. This awareness is particularly important in a democratic society such as ours in which people enter into public debate to determine the common good. Those with whom one disagrees should not be regarded as enemies but rather as people whose views deserve careful examination and may shed light on one's own.

Thomas Jefferson once said that "difference of opinion leads to inquiry, and inquiry to truth." Jefferson, a broadly educated man, argued that "if a nation expects to be ignorant and free . . . it expects what never was and never will be." As individuals and as a nation, it is imperative that we consider the opinions of others and examine them with skill and discernment. The *Opposing Viewpoints* series is intended to help readers achieve this goal.

David L. Bender and Bruno Leone,
Founders

Introduction

> "At certain times, national service is held out as a civic ideal against which all other public activities can be measured; at other times, it is a marginal factor dismissed as irrelevant or utopian."
>
> *Charles C. Moskos,*
> *sociology professor, quoted in*
> A Call to Civic Service

Two deep-seated but conflicting American traits have framed the national service debate throughout American history. While Americans believe passionately that helping others is important, they also value personal freedom and self-reliance. Alexis de Tocqueville, a French aristocrat who toured the United States in the 1830s, noted that Americans freely and voluntarily gather to help meet community needs and social goals. He published his observations about the young nation in the oft-cited two-volume book *Democracy in America* (1835 and 1840). Indeed, many essays on the topic of volunteerism quote Tocqueville, who said, "Americans of all ages, all stations in life, and all types of dispositions are forever forming associations." Volunteerism is "in the national DNA,"[1] says Matthew Spalding of the Heritage Foundation. Many Americans believe that democracy depends on vigorous civic participation. From Benjamin Franklin's fire brigade to John F. Kennedy's Peace Corps and from Franklin D. Roosevelt's New Deal work programs to George H.W. Bush's Thousand Points of Light, Americans have demonstrated throughout history the belief that service is part of the glue that holds the nation together—uniting Americans to serve a common purpose.

1. Matthew Spalding, "Compulsory National Service Would Undermine the American Character," *USA Today*, October 19, 2010.

Even Tocqueville noted, however, that the American sense of individualism sometimes came into conflict with its sense of community spirit. Thus, while Tocqueville did believe strongly in the value of voluntary association, those who oppose national service argue that he was not likely to have approved of government-sponsored service. Indeed, Tocqueville writes, "The more [government] stands in the place of associations, the more will individuals, losing the notion of combining together, require its assistance." Those who oppose government involvement in national service hold this view. Government-sponsored national service programs, whether supported through taxation or by mandate, Spalding notes, "do not encourage sacrificial giving of time and resources, which has the character-forming effect of teaching compassionate responsibility. . . . Such government-directed 'volunteerism,' by encouraging individuals and associations to look to the state as the provider of assistance, belittles authentic volunteerism."[2] This conflict between the spirit of giving and self-reliance has appeared over the years in the voices of those on both sides of the national service debate.

The first major national service program was established during the Great Depression. Unemployment rates reached 25 percent in the United States. Farmers suffered when crop prices fell by as much as 60 percent, and with little demand, jobs that depended on mining, logging, or manufacturing were scarce.

In 1932, Americans elected Franklin D. Roosevelt, who promised to put Americans back to work. Roosevelt was not interested in the dole—giving handouts to the unemployed. He believed that Americans wanted to work for their money. One of the programs he created in the early days of his presidency was the Civilian Conservation Corps (CCC). Roosevelt's CCC combined two of his philosophies: the need to put young men to work and the need to protect America's resources. The

2. *Ibid.*

program had enormous popular support and is credited with improving millions of acres of federal and state lands. CCC workers built new roads, strung new telephone lines, and planted trees. They erected fire towers, created drainage systems to improve damaged farmland, and built campgrounds with picnic shelters, swimming pools, fireplaces, and restrooms. These workers also fought forest fires and provided emergency help during floods in the Midwest. Between 1933 and 1942, Roosevelt had put 2.5 million unemployed young Americans to work.

Roosevelt's program was so successful that he called for a national service law to put people to work to support the war effort during World War II. Roosevelt and the law's supporters argued that it was the best way to eliminate the double standard of drafting young men into the military "while leaving civilians free to do almost exactly as they choose,"[3] the editors of *Life* magazine wrote in a January 24, 1944, editorial. Despite the success of the CCC, Congress blocked the proposal, primarily due to opposition from labor organizations. They argued that a "work or fight" program was unfair. Paying lower national service wages to workers would counter the hard-won efforts of those fighting for fair standards and labor practices, labor leaders maintained. Others suggested that such a law was akin to involuntary servitude. *Life* quoted Senator Robert Rice Reynolds of North Carolina who called the law a plan for "enslaving the American people." The same rhetoric can be seen in the national service debates of today.

In his inaugural address, delivered on January 20, 1961, President John F. Kennedy asked all Americans to join what he called a historic effort to fight tyranny, poverty, disease, and war. In an oft-cited quote, he called on Americans to "ask not what your country can do for you; ask what you can do for your country." Kennedy believed that it was important to establish positive relationships with developing nations so that

---

3. "The President's Message," *Life*, January 24, 1944.

they would not fall to communism. To create these relationships, he envisioned a Peace Corps. The 1961 law that established the government-run volunteer program states its purpose: "to promote world peace and friendship through a Peace Corps, which shall make available to interested countries and areas men and women of the United States qualified for service abroad and willing to serve, under conditions of hardship if necessary." At its peak in 1966, the Peace Corps put 15,556 Americans to work in developing nations worldwide.

In the late 1960s, John F. Kennedy's brother, Robert Kennedy, sought to expand the Peace Corps and its goals. Peace Corps cofounder and former senator Harris Wofford recalls, "In one of his last interviews, Robert Kennedy said he thought the Peace Corps idea should become part of the whole of life, not just a passing episode for a relative handful of people."[4] Support came from military leaders as well. In a 1966 speech, Defense Secretary Robert S. McNamara once again took up the idea of universal national service. Like Roosevelt, he argued that the inequity of having only a minority of eligible young men drafted into the military could be rectified by "asking every young person in the United States to give two years of service to his country—whether in one of the military services, in the Peace Corps or in some other volunteer development work at home or abroad."[5] Like those who oppose the high cost of national service programs today, the White House defeated national service proposals in the 1960s due to the mounting costs of the Vietnam War.

The argument that national service is vital to America was renewed once again in the 1980s. Eminent sociologists Charles C. Moskos and Morris Janowitz both favored the ideal of citizen service. They recommended a proposal that linked federal aid for higher education to voluntary national service, which would include either military reserve duty or civilian work.

4. Harris Wofford, *Of Kennedys and Kings.* University of Pittsburgh Press, 1992.
5. *Ibid.*

They called their proposal a GI bill for national service. In a June 1980 *Bulletin of the Atomic Scientists* editorial, Moskos and Janowitz wrote, "A citizen's obligation ought to become part of growing up in America." They argued that citizen service is necessary to restore the balance between citizenship rights and obligations and to promote patriotism. Like-minded analysts agreed, claiming that a sense of civic duty was experienced by too few Americans. According to a 1986 study conducted by Richard Danzig and Peter Szanton, "Military veterans, Peace Corps alumni and, ironically, immigrants, are now virtually the only Americans who experience a sense of citizenship earned rather than simply received."[6] National service, they maintain, could create that sense of citizenship.

National service did indeed become part of the national vocabulary during the 1990s, and the fervor has continued into the new millennium. President George H.W. Bush signed a law in 1990 that created a Commission on National and Community Service that evolved into the federal agency now called the Corporation for National and Community Service. His national service vision was conceived when, during his campaign, he called for Americans to become a thousand points of light through volunteer work. During his administration, President Bill Clinton endorsed and expanded Bush's efforts. In his acceptance speech at the Democratic National Convention on July 16, 1992, the then presidential candidate Clinton called for a season of service. "Just think of it: millions of energetic young men and women serving their country by teaching children, policing the streets, caring for the sick, working with the elderly or people with disabilities, building homes for the homeless, helping children to stay off drugs and out of gangs—giving us all a real sense of home and limitless possibilities." During his term, AmeriCorps sent out its first twenty thousand volunteers, and Clinton signed the Na-

6. Richard Danzig and Peter Szanton, *National Service: What Would It Mean?* Ford Foundation, 1986.

tional and Community Service Trust Act, which provided education funds for those who performed national service.

George W. Bush followed with his endorsement of national service in 2002. Following the terrorist attacks of September 11, 2001, many Americans wanted to serve the cause of freedom, and if they could not do so in the military, they wanted to serve at home. Surprising both his critics and supporters, Bush proposed to support and expand AmeriCorps and created the USA Freedom Corps to match volunteers with opportunities. In his State of the Union Address on January 29, 2002, Bush said, "My call tonight is for every American to commit at least two years—four thousand hours over the rest of your lifetime—to the service of your neighbors and your nation." In 2006, however, not unlike the national service programs of the past, his programs were constrained by the cost of the war in the Middle East and the devastation caused by Hurricane Katrina. During the second half of the Bush administration, Congress significantly cut funding for the Corporation for National and Community Service.

National service was an important issue during the 2008 presidential campaign. Both Barack Obama and John McCain vowed to support national service programs. While McCain joked that he would be glad to spend some money, however, he made clear that he would rely primarily on private industry and volunteer organizations. Obama's vision was more expansive. To explain his goal, during his campaign, Obama asked Americans to remember the outpouring of patriotism and the desire to serve that occurred after the September 11 terrorist attacks. At a forum on national service at Columbia University on September 11, 2008, Obama asked, "How do we recreate that spirit—not just during times of tragedy, not just during 9/11—how do we honor those who died and those who sacrificed—the firefighters and police officers—how do we honor them every day?" He added, "The country yearns for that, the country is hungry for it, and what has been missing is a president and a White House that taps into that in a serious way."

Obama largely kept his promise to tap into the spirit of national service. On April 21, 2009, he signed the Edward M. Kennedy Serve America Act, which reauthorized and expanded national service programs administered by the Corporation for National and Community Service. Like Roosevelt, Obama hoped to put Americans suffering from the current economic crisis to work through national service. Some believe, however, that his call for "universal" national service opened the door to criticism. Not unlike those who opposed national service programs in the 1930s and the 1960s, critics fear Obama's goal is to enslave Americans to promote his social policies. Some argue that the act will create armies of government volunteers to advance a liberal agenda. Others liken the federal funding of service learning to the youth enlistment programs used by Adolf Hitler.

Clearly the national service debate is far from over. These two camps—those that believe national service should be a civic obligation and those that contend national service abridges freedom—continue to take a firm stand. In the following chapters, the authors of the viewpoints in *Opposing Viewpoints: National Service* reflect these and other views as they explore the nature and scope of national service and what role the government should play: Is National Service Necessary? What Is the Social Impact of National Service? What Role Should Service Learning Play in Society? What Role Should the Government Play in National Service? As Tocqueville noted, Americans struggle to find a balance between their often-conflicting values: the desire to help their neighbors and a fierce sense of self-reliance. Whether any national service program can reconcile these values remains to be seen.

CHAPTER 1

Is National Service Necessary?

Chapter Preface

In many nations, military service is mandatory. In Denmark, Germany, and Norway, for example, young men are obliged to serve in the military for at least eighteen months. Pacifists or conscientious objectors who choose not to serve in the military must spend the same amount of time in civilian service to the nation. In the years since 1973, when Congress ended mandatory military service in the United States, some American analysts have been calling to reinstate mandatory military service, more commonly called the draft. Congress has thus far not heeded this call, and the United States continues to maintain an all-volunteer military force. As military needs have grown in the United States due to the wars in the Middle East, however, calls for reinstating the draft have reemerged with more fervor. Indeed, one of the more heated controversies in the debate over the necessity of national service is whether a draft is needed to defend the nation. Arguments for and against the draft in many ways mirror the debate over the necessity of all forms of national service.

Those who support the draft argue that the shared sacrifice that comes from military service would in turn create a shared sense of national purpose. According to leadership and public policy professor Hodding Carter and attorney and author Ronald Goldfarb, "We are proud of having served our country. It carved a few years out of our lives in the 1950s and '60s, but strengthened our understanding of the country we served and the people with whom we served."[1] Like-minded commentators claim that in a democratic society, the defense of the nation should be a responsibility that is equitably shared. Thus, they reason, without a universal military service requirement, those who serve and in some cases make the

---

1. Hodding Carter and Ronald Goldfarb, "An Opportunity for Shared Sacrifice," *USA Today*, October 26, 2006.

ultimate sacrifice for their country are not representative of the nation. Stanford history professor David M. Kennedy writes that "a preponderant majority of Americans with no risk whatsoever of exposure to military service has in effect hired some of the least advantaged of their fellow countrymen to do some of their most dangerous business while they go on with their affairs unbloodied and undistracted."[2]

Those who oppose the draft disagree with this characterization of the all-volunteer military in the United States. In fact, opponents assert, even when the draft was in effect, the military has never been reflective of the general population. Currently, claims Walter Y. Oi, an economics professor who served on President Richard M. Nixon's Commission on an All-Volunteer Armed Force, America's all-volunteer force has a greater percentage of high school graduates than the general population, contrary to claims that recruit quality is declining. Moreover, he maintains, predictions following the end of the draft that the defense of the nation would be borne by the blood of an all-black infantry proved false. In truth, the *Wall Street Journal* reports, most of those on the front lines are white. Studies show that a majority of African Americans who volunteer actually choose occupational specialties that will improve their chances of being promoted and retained. Draft opponents also dispute the claim that a draft is egalitarian. They argue that service, even military service, is not democratic if it is compulsory. Thus, they reason, the only true way to equitably staff a military is with volunteers. "Maintaining freedom of occupational choice and relying on incentives to attract qualified individuals for our national defense," Oi asserts, "is surely the most equitable method of procuring military manpower."[3]

2. David M. Kennedy, "The Wages of a Mercenary Army," *American Academy of Arts and Sciences Bulletin*, Spring 2006.
3. *Ibid.*

Whether a military draft is necessary to equitably and ad-equately defend the nation remains contentious. The conflict-ing values reflected in this debate are also reflected in the con-troversies explored by the authors in the following chapter. Whether national service should be a necessary civic responsi-bility for all Americans will inform policy in the United States for years to come.

> "National Service can cultivate a deep
> commitment to one's fellow citizens and
> to the country as a whole."

National Service Furthers American Ideals

Peter Frumkin and Brendan Miller

Based on interviews with national policy and thought leaders, Peter Frumkin and Brendan Miller maintain that national service furthers American ideals. According to Frumkin and Miller, national service encourages active citizenship and promotes personal growth. Moreover, they argue, national service builds social capital—social networks and trust that can improve life in American communities. National service volunteers also meet important social needs by providing low-cost public services, the authors maintain. Frumkin is director of the RGK Center for Philanthropy and Community Service at the University of Texas. Miller, once an AmeriCorps volunteer, studies democratic participation at the community level.

As you read, consider the following questions:

1. In which Roosevelt-era program does the institutionalized service movement have its roots?

Peter Frumkin and Brendan Miller, "Visions of National Service," *Society*, vol. 45, 2008, pp. 436–443. Reproduced with kind permission from Springer Science and Business Media and the author.

2. How might an attitude of generalized reciprocity impact national service members, in the authors' view?

3. Why do the authors assert that national service programs are ideal vehicles for forging networks of ties that link people together?

The USA has a long and rich history of citizens engaging in volunteerism and rendering service to their community. When Alexis de Tocqueville[1] toured America in the early nineteenth century, he commented on the American spirit of voluntary effort for the common good. As early as 1910, Americans envisioned citizen-service on a national scale. With roots in Franklin D. Roosevelt's Civilian Conservation Corps in the 1930s and 1940s, an institutionalized service movement has developed and grown over time. In the 1960s, the Economic Opportunity Act expanded domestic national service with the creation of Volunteers in Service to America (VISTA), the National Teacher Corps, and the Neighborhood Youth Corps. More recently, the National and Community Service Trust Act of 1993 furthered the national service movement by creating the Corporation for National and Community Service, a public agency that provides Americans of all ages and backgrounds with opportunities to serve their communities. The act also established AmeriCorps, a large-scale national service program that places young people in full-time, community service positions across the country. These many efforts to develop a programmatic structure around the idea of service have resulted in a long debate about what the goal of national service really ought to be.

To help us begin to understand the many ways in which national service has been conceptualized, we conducted 48 1- to 2-h [hour] interviews with policy and practice leaders in the field of national service across the country. We asked

---

1. Alexis de Tocqueville, a French philosopher and historian, penned *Democracy in America* after he traveled throughout the United States in 1831.

people to explain what they thought the fundamental purpose and rationale for national service might be. . . . The conversations we had slowly began to fall into a recognizable pattern, in which four core visions or conceptions of the purpose and impact of national service emerged. These conceptions were distilled from interviews with program staff at large AmeriCorps-supported programs and small community-based programs in both urban and rural locations around the country, as well as with leading thinkers and researchers, notable national service critics and those involved in crafting the 1993 legislation and implementing it at the Corporation for National [and Community] Service. The four conceptions presented here represent the framing that demonstrates the greatest consistency and economy in relation to the analysis we did of the content of our conversations.

National Service as Citizenship

National service and citizenship are often closely linked. Those who think of national service as citizenship development hope that service will render participants more informed and engaged. However, in the same way that there are many ways to conceptualize the goal of national service, there are a variety of ways to understand what makes a good citizen. We can think of citizenship as consisting in a number of interconnected dimensions, including the recognition and appreciation of a set of legal rights and obligations, the fulfillment of democratic responsibilities, and commitment to country and fellow citizens.

Not all these dimensions of citizenship are necessarily tied up in the idea of national service. Several of our interview subjects acknowledged that national service may not directly contribute to a greater understanding of, and appreciation for, constitutional rights and responsibilities. AmeriCorps, for example, does not require its programs to educate their members about these rights and responsibilities. There is no curriculum on what it means to be a citizen that is part of national service programs. Furthermore, AmeriCorps explicitly prohibits members from engaging in political activities (e.g., working with a political party). All these constraints aside, we heard that national service still can be a potent laboratory for learning what it means to be a citizen. Volunteers may get a sense of responsibilities as citizens simply by virtue of acting to help others, observing the power of politics to transform a community, or learning about an issue and growing committed to addressing it through policy change.

Learning Civic Habits

National service may also cultivate a sense of generalized reciprocity, making members more inclined to seek to exercise their rights and uphold their responsibilities after their year of service has been completed. Through the giving and receiving that occurs in service and through interacting with local community-based institutions, members learn civic habits that translate to higher levels of public institutions. National service promotes critical citizenship primarily by exposing members to injustice and systemic failures they would not otherwise experience firsthand, which can lead to future citizen action. As one observer noted: "Privileged kids come face to face with individuals whose needs aren't being met. And realizing that causes them to question, well what kind of society is this? They were actually moved by the belief that the system ought to work and it wasn't working for some people." . . .

Citizenship can also be cultivated when individuals are empowered and made to believe that their engagement and participation can make a difference. National service increases the appetite of volunteers for change and tends to attract young people interested in making a difference. An AmeriCorps program manager commented about the energizing nature of national service: "You don't come to our organization because you want to maintain the status quo and keep people oppressed regardless of your political background. You come here because you think something is wrong and there might be something you can do about it. People come here to address an issue and we can leverage that more effectively by challenging them to really commit to that original." . . .

A number of our interviewees described ways that national service can cultivate a deep commitment to one's fellow citizens and to the country as a whole. Serving together under a shared purpose can create new ties and connections to Americans one might otherwise feel alienated from. By building social capital in this way and creating a broader understanding of *us*, patriotism is also built. An alternative approach to develop a sense of patriotism is through an appreciative inquiry into what has and does make America great, which would come in the form of American history and civics lessons. It would be possible to incorporate this kind of education into national service, but it is not inherently a product of national service. . . .

Regardless of how one conceives of citizenship, our interviewees expressed confidence that national service could indeed contribute to its development. National service may not promote all dimensions of citizenship equally and it may often favor some aspects over others. In some cases, this is due simply to the nature of national service. In other cases, it is a function of particular policies and implementation decisions that could be changed or adapted to refocus service on different objectives.

National Service as Personal Growth

In its most basic form, AmeriCorps and other national service programs start with the input of discounted labor when young people commit to work in community service positions for modest stipends. In reality, the real starting point of service is the impulse to help that young people have. One reason why people volunteer is an earnest desire to do something socially useful and to help others. There is a second reason for volunteering, which is connected neither to the urgency of community needs nor to the nature of the social commitments of volunteers: Many people are drawn into volunteering and helping work because it is a way for them to enact their values and live out their convictions.

It is not hard to think about national service in terms of the personal growth it generates for those it touches, particularly the volunteers, but also including nonprofit staff working alongside the volunteers and community members who come in contact with these young people. Service creates an opportunity to work on problems of public concern and participate in the lives of others—whose paths one might otherwise never cross—in a structured and supportive environment. As they experience making a difference for others, volunteers or corps members, as they are sometimes termed, grow and mature, and also develop new skills and talents. National service imbues participants with benefits that far exceed the meager financial stipends that often accompany service. Those who participate in service benefit from a broadened perspective on work and life, the development of workplace skills, and greater awareness of public issues.

A Culture of Idealism

One reason personal growth can be achieved through service is that many AmeriCorps programs are animated by a culture of idealism. Young people often apply to and then join national service programs because they believe, or at least [are] open to the possibility, that they can make a difference in the world. Through a selection bias for these idealistic individuals and against hardened cynics, a culture of idealism grows around the programs. It is also worth noting that most AmeriCorps members are young adults, who are on average more idealistic than their elders before they serve. Still this culture of idealism contributes to creativity and innovation because there is a greater openness to try new things, or to try old things a second time. A program manager with experience working with AmeriCorps commented: "What I've seen with having younger folks involved is a high degree of energy—an ability and a desire to work hard. You'll see young people really tackle work that others don't want to do, and bring enthusiasm to that." She continued on to point out that as part of the process of recruiting and motivating your people, it is essential to stress the larger vision. In her organization's case, it was the goal of eliminating substandard housing. When this is done, volunteers work hard because they enjoy chasing after a vision or goal and are generally less cynical. They see themselves as part of something larger and enjoy the potential to deepen their understanding of the world and their role in it. . . .

The idea that service enlarges vision and develops skills is held deeply by most proponents of service. It is part of the rationale that they have constructed for the often difficult and challenging work of engaging young people in public problem solving over the course of an entire year. AmeriCorps brings out the best in a community and individuals and invites people to serve for perhaps the first time. People who in the past may have been consumers of service, an AmeriCorps member is now able to invite them to step from the sidelines and be a full contributor even if they never thought they could serve their communities in a significant way. This creates a feeling of self-worth and builds self-esteem. The promise of individual growth is also important to participants. It provides some of the attraction of national service. One program director who originally served as a member had this to say: "People are willing to sacrifice a year of their lives and live on a pittance if they can say, 'Wow! I really grew from that in a way that I would not have been able to if I just worked for that organization and I think it's worth it.' That's certainly why I'm still here."

National Service as Social Capital

Different from either human or financial capital, social capital refers to "features of social organization, such as networks, norms, and trust, which facilitate coordination and cooperation for mutual benefit." The existence of social capital has important consequences for the quality of civic engagement and politics. Although the idea of trust is an old one, it has in recent years become a powerful organizing concept for researchers studying markets and politics. . . .

In many ways, national service programs are ideal vehicles for forging networks of ties that link people together. Service has a unique role to play in forging the ties that link people together in ways that allow them to accomplish collective tasks. In the process of meeting to form a neighborhood crime patrol or in volunteering at the local shelter, individuals make new acquaintances that can be useful for some time to come. The relationships and ties created by the pursuit of common purposes may seem rather pedestrian at the time they are being constructed. Working together with residents to put together a youth sports program for a poor community may seem like an unremarkable activity for AmeriCorps members to undertake. However, this kind of work forges linkages, and soon individuals see one another in public space and begin to match names and faces. Thus, when it comes to enticing people outside their narrow networks of family and friends, service at the community level can be a powerful instrument for the forging of relationships, which may invigorate individuals' interest in public life and create trust where once there was none.

Connecting Organizations and Communities

While social capital and trust may seem like things that adhere only to individuals, they can and do connect organizations and communities together. Social capital can be built

A Way to Keep the Republic

At this moment in our history, 220 years after the Constitutional Convention, the way to get citizens involved in civic life, the way to create a common culture that will make a virtue of our diversity, the way to give us that more capacious sense of "we"—finally, the way to keep the Republic—is universal national service. No, not mandatory or compulsory service but service that is in our enlightened self-interest as a nation. We are at a historic junction; . . . it is time for the next president to mine the desire that is out there for serving and create a program for universal national service. . . . It is the simple but compelling idea that devoting a year or more to national service, whether military or civilian, should become a countrywide rite of passage, the common expectation and widespread experience of virtually every young American.

Richard Stengel, "A Time to Serve," Time, August 30, 2007.

through collaborations between organizations and joint service delivery efforts that rally entire communities toward a common goal. This sort of community-wide social capital was mentioned by many of the people we spoke with, a number of whom noted that these collaborations and connections were not always planned intentionally but emerged organically through running their national service program. One program director and academic talked about the impact his program had within his university. "Our AmeriCorps program brought together people from different parts of the university who would not have come together otherwise, to work on common projects. This creates cross-fertilization." One concern about social capital is that it may be ephemeral and require lots of regular maintenance. In the case of this university-centered project, the connections and relationship outlasted even the formal presence of the national service project: "Each part of the university that participated was represented on a campus coordinating committee, which was unprecedented at my university. It brought together different service efforts and became a vehicle for future collaborative projects, even though our AmeriCorps program is no longer funded." National service can thus be seen as a tool for building social capital within large clusters of institutions and across entire communities.

The vision of national service that focuses on social capital formation tended to be embraced by those who felt uncomfortable with narrow boundaries around the potential impact of these programs. In fact, when stripped down to its essential elements, one observer noted: "I am not convinced that there is something unique about the work that gets done [through national service], that is significantly different than typical volunteer work." This expert went on to note that the real contribution of AmeriCorps lies "in the more unique opportunity to build bridging social capital and to change the norms regarding what is expected of citizens." This broader conception of the purpose of service represents the core of the vision of national service as social capital builder.

National Service as Public Work

Far less complex and contingent than the concept of social capital is the idea of public work. In its most basic terms, national service has long been about meeting critical public needs and filling gaps created by government and market failures. Volunteers are part of a system designed to deliver at low cost important public services that otherwise would not be available to communities. National service is believed to be an alternative means of addressing public needs without reliance on traditional forms of contracting or direct public-service employment. In all these functions, service is a form of production and a low-cost way of meeting critical needs, particularly in the focus areas of education, human services, environment, and public safety. Most people think about national service in terms of the simple instrumental ends it accomplishes. The slogan adopted by the Corporation [for National and Community Service] for conveying this vision was "getting things done," a notion that was emphasized during the early years [of] AmeriCorps. This emphasis was at least partly a matter of political expediency. Under pressure to show that the expense of national service was producing something of value for taxpayers, the Corporation spent a great deal of time and expense documenting for Congress what was in fact getting done. Counting the number of shrubs planted by a service project or documenting the number of hours of tutoring delivered is much easier to track and communicate than a changed level of civic engagement, a significant improvement in terms of participants' personal growth, or increased social capital formation. But the attraction of defining national service in terms of what it gets done reflects the broader debate in which we find ourselves immersed. There has long been a tension in American society between those who see citizenship from the lens of civic education, identity development and patriotism and those who conceive of it in terms of what results are achieved. The later perspective has grown in popularity in recent years, as the former has slipped in credibility due to a lack of good evidence and empirical data to support its plausibility.

Getting Things Done

To understand national service in terms of what it concretely accomplishes for communities and the nation is simple and straightforward enough. The immediate, direct results of the service undertaken are the most visible and the most easily comprehensible to people within and outside the service movement. It can be documented whether certain intended outputs are being produced and the costs of producing these outputs are also identifiable. Outputs or units of service, e.g., number of empty lots cleared of garbage or number of elderly persons served meals at home, can be measured and tracked, and even aggregated across communities. Given the apparent uncertainty in measuring the other impacts of national service and the inherent importance of building support for the work being undertaken, a number of the people we spoke with felt it was entirely appropriate to conceive of national service in large measure along these instrumental terms. Still, some we spoke with hesitated to focus on these instrumental achievements, drawing a distinction between *outputs*, which track short-term units of service delivered, and *outcomes*, which are broader and more complex units of analysis. At the end of this debate about what can be measured and what is worth measuring, there still remains the basic question of what does national service actually accomplish for communities or the nation. . . .

Beyond perhaps serving as the stepping-stone for the achievement of the other ends of national service, the public work conception has an additional dimension. Getting things done may involve actually delivering a certain amount of service to a community, but it can also mean building the capacity of the organizations in the community so that they can "get things done." In this sense, the instrumental vision of national service has both direct and indirect components. The direct component involves using volunteers to actually do the work while the indirect component depends on nonprofit capacity building to get things done on a larger and lasting scale, even after specific service initiatives end or national service slots move to other communities. Evidence is growing that AmeriCorps does indeed impact the hosting nonprofits and more and more people believe these effects to be significant. Capacity building has also been an explicit priority under President [George W.] Bush, which helps to raise awareness of what was already happening and to further align programs with this goal. The underlying logic of capacity building as the anchor of public work is that by developing the capacity of the nonprofit sector and bringing effective initiatives to scale, one can increase the ability of the sector to respond effectively to important national needs, thus benefiting us all.

Thus, what at first glance appeared to be obvious—counting what gets accomplished through service—turns out to be more complex. Part of the complexity relates to the fact that the process of getting things done involves not just the production of community benefits, but also the construction of capacity and the leveraging of additional resources outside national service. In this sense, the public work conception is linked to other intervening conceptions of service which are broader than the simple question of how many midnight basketball games were organized in a given community to help keep young people from getting into trouble. It is about everything that happens around the game and what this means for the community over the long haul.

Why National Service?

The four main visions of national service that we defined from our many conversations may not completely exhaust all the possible visions of national service. However, they do reflect the full range of the perspectives that were articulated to us. We think that no matter whether one is a proponent or opponent of the idea of service, getting clear about what these programs are intended to accomplish is important. By setting out four core visions of national service, we hope that policy makers and practitioners can continue to think about the relationships among these objectives, to prioritize at the local level those that are most essential, and to design and implement future national service programs to maximize all or some of these four intended impacts.

| *"In a putatively free society there is something wrong with universal national service even if it is voluntary."*

National Service Does Not Further American Ideals

Sheldon Richman

Sheldon Richman, editor of the libertarian journal the Freeman, *argues in the following viewpoint that universal national service is inappropriate in a free society. Universal national service, in which the government forces American citizens to participate actively or through taxation, is not voluntary, he asserts. Even if proponents could prove that citizens should be involved in civic life or that promoting a common culture is necessary, the government should not be the instrument of these goals, Richman claims. Universal national service is not about people doing good deeds for those who need help but rather about service to the nation, which contravenes democratic principles, he reasons.*

As you read, consider the following questions:

1. Why does Richman assert that atomistic individualism is more than a straw man used to discredit liberalism?

Sheldon Richman, "The Goal Is Freedom: The Nation as an Object of Service," *Freeman*, September 7, 2007. Reproduced by permission. www.thefreemanonline.org.

2. What does the author think would have been a better question to have asked Benjamin Franklin after the Constitutional Convention?

3. In the author's view, how do ancient and modern notions of liberty differ?

What distinguishes the libertarian[1] (liberal) spirit from its alternative is the conviction that free individuals who respect one another's sovereignty will generate and sustain a benevolent prosperous social order without direction from a central bureaucratic authority. Atomistic individualism[2] never had anything to do with genuine liberalism, which is a social philosophy that looks to the cooperation inherent in the division of labor and free exchange to deliver its material and nonmaterial benefits. The market—the realm of consent, contract, and mutual accommodation—always was thought to include nonpecuniary relationships.

Those who see heavy-handed government as the indispensable antidote for atomistic individualism have long beat up on that pathetic straw man. But atomistic individualism is something more than a straw man useful in the attempt to discredit liberalism. The critics of liberalism seem sincerely to believe that without a strong central authority, society would degenerate and dissolve, as though mere people—as opposed to leaders—are too benighted to fend for themselves. In this alternative worldview, centralized power is the glue that binds us together. For the liberal, no such glue was needed. The advantages of individualism embedded in social cooperation— call it molecular individualism—are too obvious to be overlooked. (Children spontaneously discover the gains from trade at an early age.) That shows how great the chasm is between real liberalism and all forms of illiberalism.

1. The term liberal, which in modern thought often refers to left-leaning political ideals, originally referred to the ideal of individual rights. Today, libertarian ideals refer to individual liberties and support of the free market.
2. Atomistic individualism is the belief in the self-sufficiency of the individual.

Examining Universal National Service

One can readily see illiberalism all around. In the [August 30, 2007] issue of *Time* magazine, Richard Stengel, the magazine's managing editor, calls for universal national service in his article "A Time to Serve". Stengel says the program he has in mind would be voluntary, not mandatory. Americans don't like to be told what they have to do; many have argued that requiring service drains the gift of its virtue. It would be based on carrots, not sticks—"doing well by doing good," as Benjamin Franklin, the true father of civic engagement, put it.

Let's be thankful for Stengel's wish not to compel anyone to participate. This is good for two reasons. The obvious one is that forced service is slavery, even if it is temporary. By what right could the individuals constituting the government *require* people to perform civilian or military tasks? What do those Fourth of July platitudes mean if we are to have compulsory labor? That this could even be suggested in a society that considers itself free only shows what strangers many thinkers are to reason.

Stengel's voluntarism is also good because it lets us examine the essence of his proposal without getting sidetracked on the issue of compulsion. In a putatively free society there is something wrong with universal national service even if it is voluntary.

One more thing to clear out of the way: Stengel's program is not entirely voluntary. Those who would pay for it would have no choice in the matter because it would be financed through taxation—i.e., fiscal force. For example, he wants the government to invest $5,000 for every baby born. When a person reaches 18 he or she could have the money and interest but only by pledging to do a year's civilian or military service. That's one of the carrots of which he speaks. (The money could only be used for school, starting a business, or buying a house.) Stengel may believe there is no better use of our money than to pay for his service program, but many of us will respectfully disagree.

Restoring the Republic

Stengel begins with the over-told story of Benjamin Franklin's admonition to a woman who, after the Constitutional Convention, asked if the country was to be a monarchy or a republic. A republic, if you can keep it, Franklin replied. (There it's been told yet again. A better question would have been, Why did you scrap the perfectly good Articles of Confederation, Dr. Franklin. We've had 13 small republics running acceptably well for eight years. Not enough central government for you?) Stengel continues:

> But at this moment in our history, 220 years after the Constitutional Convention, the way to get citizens involved in civic life, the way to create a common culture that will make a virtue of our diversity, the way to give us that more capacious sense of we—finally, the way to keep the Republic—is universal national service. No, not mandatory or compulsory service but service that is in our enlightened self-interest as a nation. We are at a historic junction; with the first open presidential election in more than a half-century, it is time for the next president to mine the desire that is out there for serving and create a program for universal national service that will be his—or her—legacy for decades to come. It is the simple but compelling idea that devoting a year or more to national service, whether military or civilian, should become a countrywide rite of passage, the common expectation and widespread experience of virtually every young American.

Where to begin? We might start by pointing out that the discussion ought to be directed not to *keeping* the republic but *restoring* it. I don't know what Stengel's been doing for the last, oh, couple centuries, but this ain't the republic it used to be. (And maybe it never was.) When you consider the flow of power to Washington and, within Washington, to the executive branch, what we have looks more and more like an elective monarchy than a republic. Add to this the incumbent-

Humble Servants of Society

Instead of being sent to coal and iron mines and the frames of skycrapers, young Americans will be sent to assemble solar panels and windmills and hybrid plug-in cars, in addition to mentoring children of the poor and cleaning up public spaces and keeping the elderly company—many of them lured by the carrot of college tuition. . . . Americans will be expected to become humble servants of society and believers in causes "higher than themselves," especially the one that demands that restitution and reparations be paid to a despoiled planet. And if not enough Americans "volunteer" to serve, they can be made to [by] . . . direct conscription, or a special tax . . . to fund the $5.7 billion national service price tag of the [Edward M. Kennedy Serve America Act].

Edward Cline, *"Obama's 'Blood-Tax': Compulsory 'National Service' Revisited,"* Capitalism, *May 18, 2009.*

protection system and the untouchable regulatory fourth branch, and any resemblance to a republic is almost entirely cosmetic.

The Role of Government

Stengel is quite certain that universal national service is the way to get citizens involved in civil life, create a common culture, and give us that more capacious sense of "we." But he should have first demonstrated 1) that we need those things done and 2) that government is the instrument for doing them. Before the quote above, Stengel writes, "There had been only a handful of other republics in all of human history, and most were small and far away. The founders' pessimism, though, came not from history but from their knowledge of human nature. A republic, to survive, needed not only the consent of the governed but also their active participation. It was not a machine that would go of itself; free societies do not stay free without the involvement of their citizens."

There's always a danger in talking about the founders. They were not a homogeneous group. Whom does Stengel have in mind, [Thomas] Jefferson or [Alexander] Hamilton? Patrick Henry or James Madison? The Federalists or the Anti-Federalists? The more libertarian of the founders would agree that a republic isn't a machine on autopilot. But the involvement they had in mind was more along the lines of eternal vigilance (the phrase is the Irishman John Philpot Curran's), jealousy (Jefferson), and localism, not whatever Stengel means by national service. The object of involvement was the preservation of liberty by keeping power caged, not the engineering of a common culture through government-managed associations.

A Prophetic Warning

As Stengel laments the detachment of the average American from the affairs of the republic, he might reread (or, more likely, *read*) the Anti-Federalist papers, for the critics of the proposed Constitution (consolidation) warned prophetically that a large territorial republic, as opposed to a confederation of small republics, was unviable, worked against popular participation, and would likely end in tyranny and empire. As Pennsylvania Minority put it in 1787,

> [I]t is the opinion of the most celebrated writers on government, and confirmed experience, that a very extensive territory cannot be governed on the principles of freedom, otherwise than by a confederation of republics, possessing all the powers of internal government; but united in the management of their general, and foreign concerns. . . . [S]hould it be demonstrated, that the powers vested by this constitution in Congress, will have such an effect as necessarily to

produce one consolidated government, the question then will be reduced to this short issue, viz., whether satiated with the blessings of liberty; whether repenting of the folly of so recently asserting their unalienable rights, against foreign despots at the expence of so much blood and treasure, and such painful and arduous struggles, the people of America are not willing to resign every privilege of freemen, and submit to the dominion of an absolute government, that will embrace all America in one chain of despotism; or whether they will with virtuous indignation, spurn at the shackles prepared for them, and confirm their liberties by a conduct becoming freemen.

If this view is right, then it is the height of irony to look to the central government to restore republican virtue.

Ancient Notions of Liberty

The early nineteenth-century French liberal Benjamin Constant identified a distinction that seems lost on Stengel and many others. Constant pointed out that there is an ancient notion of liberty and a modern notion of liberty. In the ancient world liberty meant participation in the [political organization], but once a collective decision was made, the individual was obliged to go along. But the modern notion makes such participation but a tiny fraction of what comprises liberty. The major part consists in the autonomy of the individual:

> It is the right of everyone to express their opinion, choose a profession and practice it, to dispose of property, and even to abuse it; to come and go without permission, and without having to account for their motives or undertakings. It is everyone's right to associate with other individuals, either to discuss their interests, or to profess the religion which they and their associates prefer, or even simply to occupy their days or hours in a way which is most compatible with their inclinations or whims.

If Stengel thinks universal service is the key to maintaining (or restoring) a republic, he is clearly an ancient. A modern, in the classical-liberal Enlightenment sense, would understand that top-down direction of people's activities is not only unnecessary to civil society but inimical to it. State demands on individuals are anathema to the liberal outlook. . . .

Collectivism and Nationalism

I hope I won't be accused of exaggerating Stengel's position. Read his own words: "[T]he next president can harness the spirit of volunteerism that already exists and make it a permanent part of American culture. . . . [T]he next president—whatever party—should set a goal to enlist at least 1 million Americans annually in national service by the year 2016."

Pardon, but the words president and harness in the same sentence make me uneasy. A president has no business harnessing much of anything at all.

Americans are ready to be asked to do something, Stengel says. Who are these people waiting for the state to ask them to do something? And why should they be obliged? As we say, get a life. People who really want to do something don't wait to be asked. They do it. Stengel acknowledges that volunteerism and civic participation since the '70s are near all-time highs. So what's he going on about anyway?

Everything wrong with Stengel's proposal is summed up in his phrase universal national service. Don't misunderstand what he's saying. He's not talking about people doing good deeds for others who need help, but rather service to a quasi-mystical entity: The *Nation*. Why else does he call it national service? In Stengel's view, only through such service can citizens attain fulfillment and all of them together become a unified We. It's sheer collectivism and nationalism, the history of which isn't terribly attractive. We've heard such appeals before—Italy in the 1920s and '30s, if I'm not mistaken.

| "Faith-based and community volunteers are not only effective but they are an essential element of our nation's response to critical challenges we face at home and abroad."

National Service Addresses America's Social Problems

David L. Caprara

In the following viewpoint, David L. Caprara claims that national service addresses pressing American social problems. National service organizations such as AmeriCorps and other grassroots and faith-based groups have proven success fighting poverty, gang violence, environmental degradation, and other social problems, he maintains. For example, Caprara asserts, although studies have shown that the children of prisoners often end up in prison themselves, the Amachi mentoring program has significantly reduced that number. Volunteer service groups are closest to the problems that their communities face and are therefore better able to identify effective solutions, he reasons. Caprara, whose remarks were made before the US House Committee on Education and Labor, directs the Initiative on International Volunteering and Service at the Brookings Institution.

David L. Caprara, "Renewing America Through National Service and Volunteerism," Testimony Before the US House Committee on Education and Labor, Brookings Institution, February 25, 2009.

As you read, consider the following questions:

1. Through what type of groups do most Americans volunteer, according to Caprara?

2. What does the author claim has been one of the most effective gang intervention programs in the nation?

3. What example does the author give to support his belief that faith-based organizations are more nimble and innovative than governmental bureaucratic bodies?

I am pleased to speak about the powerful work of volunteers serving through faith-based and community organizations and the positive impacts they are having on our nation's most challenging social issues. I commend you for recognizing the potential of these dedicated volunteers.

I also applaud President Barack Obama for his signal leadership in making the cause of service a centerpiece of his presidency. His call to a new generation to give national and even global leadership in service to others has the potential to become a defining legacy of this administration.

Addressing Social Difficulties

Expanding partnerships with neighborhood mediating institutions has proven to be an effective path in addressing many of the social difficulties we face as a country.

During my service at the Corporation for National and Community Service [CNCS], I was tasked with leveling the playing field and advancing innovative service programs— VISTA [Volunteers in Service to America], AmeriCorps, Senior Corps, and Learn and Serve America. I often considered the insightful words of one of my mentors, Robert Woodson, founder and president of the Center for Neighborhood Enterprise, and author of the landmark book, *Triumphs of Joseph*.

Woodson, who has been frequently called to testify about grassroots community remedies by Congress and our nation's governors, told me that faith-based initiatives are not about promoting a particular faith, but rather, advancing secular outcomes that faith-based and other grassroots groups are uniquely positioned to effect. He notes that not only are these groups generally the closest to the problems in a community, they are the ones most often trusted by residents, particularly in times of need like our present economic crisis.

Volunteer efforts brought to bear by faith-based groups, since Tocqueville[1] first noted our nation's founding charitable traditions and social capital in the nineteenth century, have been immensely important throughout American history. In fact, according to Bureau of Labor Statistics [BLS] data, more Americans volunteer through religious groups than any other kind of organization.

Successful Faith-Based Models

A CNCS Research and Policy Development report, entitled "Volunteer Management Capacity in America's Charities and Congregations," found that volunteers can boost both the quality of services and delivery capabilities in charities and congregations while reducing costs.

We could cite many examples of successful faith-based models, such as the Latino Pastoral Action Center of Rev. Ray Rivera in the Bronx, which has made great use of AmeriCorps volunteers in building community capacity. Southeast Idaho's Retired and Senior Volunteer Initiative and the Columbus, Ohio, based Economic and Community Development Institute serving Muslim refugees from Somalia and Ethiopia, as well as Jewish and Pentecostal Christian refugees from the former Soviet Union, provide other models.

At the Corporation, we teamed up with HHS [Department of Health and Human Services] administration for Children and Families in leveraging volunteer expertise with fam-

---

1. Alexis de Tocqueville, a French philosopher and historian, penned *Democracy in America* after he traveled throughout the United States in 1831.

Tasks Performed by AmeriCorps Members
(By percentage participating)

Task	State and National (%)	National Civilian Community Corps (%)
Tutor, mentor or take care of children, teens or adults	82.3%	88.4%
Clean trails or do other environmental work	62.4	97.3
Organize or do administrative work for programs that help needy individuals	59.1	55.1
Help renovate, construct or clean offices or buildings for needy people	49.4	86.8
Help care for sick, elderly or homeless people	42.6	66.8
Work involving disaster relief	------	29.5

TAKEN FROM: Corporation for National & Community Service, "Serving Country and Community: A Longitudinal Study of Service in AmeriCorps," December 2004.

ily strengthening, fatherhood and healthy marriage programs, and economic asset development with groups like People for People founded by Rev. Herb Lusk, the former Philadelphia Eagles "praying running back." Bishop Joseph Henderson converted a former juvenile detention facility into the Bragg Hill Family Life Center in Fredericksburg, Virginia, supported by Doris Buffett's Sunshine Lady Foundation. The Potters House of Bishop TD Jakes in Dallas launched a nationwide initiative promoting responsible fatherhood and ex-offender reentry with faith-based volunteers and new media technology.

Mentoring Children of Prisoners

I would like to touch more deeply upon two innovative program models—one, the Amachi initiative, which utilizes CNCS volunteer resources, and another, the Violence Free Zone Initiative engaging former gang members and other forms of indigenous community volunteer capacity.

Researchers at the Cambridge University Institute of Criminology have shown that children of prisoners are far more likely to become involved in crime in the future than children from other backgrounds. The Amachi program, founded by former Philadelphia Mayor Rev. Wilson Goode, provides this vulnerable cohort of young people with caring adult mentors who help guide them to success in life, avoiding a pathway to incarceration, which statistics show would too often be the case without such intervention.

Amachi, whose name in Africa means, "who knows what God will bring forth from this child," began training faith-based organizations to play a key role in scaling up the program after its founding in Philadelphia in 2003, with the support of Big Brothers Big Sisters and area congregations. To date the initiative has enrolled 3,000 congregations as partners mentoring more than 100,000 children across America.

The Amachi mentoring model, supported by AmeriCorps members who assist recruitment of community volunteers and form congregational mentoring hubs, has proven so effective that it was adopted by the Department of Health and Human Services as the basis of the federal Mentoring Children of Prisoners program. At the Corporation for National and Community Service, it was our great honor to support Dr. Goode in helping to replicate the Amachi success with the help of Senior Corps, AmeriCorps, and VISTA volunteers nationwide. We then expanded that effective approach with a new initiative of VISTA and DOJ [Department of Justice] programs that built mentoring and support hubs with faith-based and community volunteers who share their love and practical transition support for ex-offenders coming home.

Promoting Violence-Free Zones

Robert Woodson's Center for Neighborhood Enterprise [CNE] has developed one of the most effective gang intervention programs in our country, by tapping indigenous community healing agents and volunteers from within crime-ridden neighborhoods. The Center reaches out to former gang members who have been transformed by faith, and connects them with other adjudicated and at-risk youths in high-crime schools and community centers.

In 1997, CNE stepped in after Darryl Hall, a twelve-year-old District boy, was shot and killed in a senseless gang war between the "Circle" and "Avenue" crews and others that had already left fifty young people dead in southeast Washington, DC. In partnership with the Alliance of Concerned Men, many who were ex-offenders themselves, CNE negotiated a truce and helped the young people involved gain skills and find jobs as an alternative to drug dealing and crime. Those young people were then engaged as ambassadors of peace in their neighborhoods, motivating other youths toward positive attitudes and behaviors. Ten years later, crew-related homicides have been eliminated in the area since the intervention began.

Today CNE is expanding the reach of Violence Free Zones [VFZ] to cities across the country including Chicago, where a major spike in gang violence threatens to cut short the lives of our young people and their fellow neighborhood residents.

Evidence of Success

Baylor University researchers, who Woodson recently cited in testimony before the House Judiciary Committee, documented the impact of the VFZ intervention model in six Milwaukee public schools where violent incidents were reduced by 32%. Suspension rates were also dramatically reduced, and student grade point averages rose compared to the control sites.

Dramatic decreases of violent incidents where CNE grassroots leaders intervened were also reported in Baltimore, Dallas, Atlanta, and Washington, DC.

Congress, the administration, and private foundations would be well served to advance dynamic linkages and partnerships with such effective grassroots, faith-based programs together with the volunteer power of the Corporation for National and Community Service and programs at the Departments of Education, Labor, and Justice. Attorney General Eric Holder could be a natural leader for such a cross-sector effort. He has been a strong proponent of Violence Free Zones since their inception during his prior tenure at Justice.

I believe these initiatives represent "low-hanging fruit" if the new White House Council on Faith-Based and Community Partnerships wants to scale up such results-oriented models with expanded private-sector and public support.

In addition to their unique quality of being deeply embedded in communities, faith-based organizations are usually much more nimble and innovative than governmental bureaucratic bodies. Take for instance the response to Hurricane Katrina. Groups like Lutheran Disaster Response, Islamic Relief USA, and the Points of Light and Interfaith Works Faith and Service Institute, directed by Rev. Mark Farr and Eric Schwarz, were able to mobilize quickly. They and countless other faith-based groups galvanized congregations, synagogues and mosques into action with donations and volunteer "boots on the ground" to help families recover, while FEMA [Federal Emergency Management Agency] and other agencies famously struggled to respond.

International Voluteering

Our nations' volunteers have also made great headway in promoting global solutions. Freedom from Terror polls have noted a marked drop in support for violent terrorism and a dramatic increase in positive views toward the United States in populous Muslim nations like Indonesia, Bangladesh and Pakistan following our national and volunteer responses after the tsunami and earthquake disasters that were sustained beyond the initial period of aid.

According to a BLS assessment report by researchers with Washington University's Center for Social Development, approximately 52% of global volunteers from America said their main volunteering organization was a religious one.

The [Initiative on] International Volunteering [and Service] at the Brookings Institution, launched at a forum with General Colin Powell nearly three years ago, has achieved solid gains in doubling a cohort from 50,000 to 100,000 international volunteers through the Building Bridges Coalition, comprised of more than 180 US-based international service NGOs [nongovernmental organizations], faith-based groups, universities and corporations.

Together with the national policy leadership, . . . the Brookings volunteering team crafted a design for a new Global Service Fellowship initiative that would empower tens of thousands of new international service volunteers supported with modest stipends that could be redeemed by NGO and faith-based entities registered with the State Department. Global Service Fellowship legislation patterned after our research has attracted broad bipartisan support. . . . Our team also helped to craft the Service Nation global volunteering platform, which calls for doubling the Peace Corps, enacting Global Service Fellowships, and authorizing Volunteers for Prosperity at USAID.

In the past year my travels have included visits to hot spots of Israel and Palestine, Kenya, at the Philippines, Brazil and other nations supporting ongoing Global Peace Festival initiatives on each continent. Through these efforts I have witnessed firsthand the tremendous power of interfaith partnerships and volunteering to heal conflicts across tribal and religious divides. Upcoming Global Peace Festival initiatives in

Mindanao, Jakarta, and other cities including an International Young Leaders Summit in Nairobi . . . hold particular promise. Over 120 global leaders, NGOs and faith-based groups have supported the call for a new Global Service Alliance in these endeavors. Such a "global peace corps" will build a vital link between volunteering and global development to impact peace-building outcomes.

In conclusion, faith-based and community volunteers are not only effective but they are an essential element of our nation's response to critical challenges we face at home and abroad. Now is the time for our national leaders and the private sector to tap into their full potential in light of our massive challenges ahead.

We have only begun to scratch the surface of the incredible wisdom and resources of transformative hope, embodied in today's grassroots "Josephs."

I hope we can rally across party lines with this president to connect and support these groups in a force for good, as proven allies in the fight against poverty and disease, gang violence, environmental degradation and global conflict and disasters. Such an alliance would show the world the full potential of America's best diplomats, our volunteers.

I would like to close by quoting Dr. [Martin Luther] King's words that my former mentor and boss Jack Kemp, the distinguished former House member and President Bush 41's HUD [US Department of Housing and Urban Development] Secretary, often cited in his testimony:

"I don't know what the future holds, but I know who holds the future."

> "[AmeriCorps] has never provided cred-
> ible evidence of benefit to the United
> States."

National Service Does Not Address Social Problems

James Bovard

In the following viewpoint, conservative author James Bovard argues that national service programs such as AmeriCorps are political, feel-good programs with little real impact on social problems. In fact, he claims, in 2003 the Office of Management and Budget found that AmeriCorps had not demonstrated any measurable results. Indeed, Bovard asserts, national service programs measure the number who serve and the amount of time served, not the actual impact of service on the community. Thus, he reasons, using taxpayer money to pay volunteers to meet needs that politicians did not believe needed direct government intervention is unsound. Bovard is author of Attention Deficit Democracy *and* Lost Rights.

As you read, consider the following questions:

1. How many American tax dollars has AmeriCorps consumed since its creation in 1993, according to Bovard?

James Bovard, "The National Service Illusion," *Ripon Forum*, vol. 42, April–May 2008, pp. 42–44. Reproduced by permission.

2. What did Leslie Lenkowsky concede about AmeriCorps after he resigned in 2003?

3. In the author's view, why are the legions of needs identified by national service advocates currently unmet?

N ational service is one of the hottest causes of presidential candidates [referring to candidates in the 2008 US presidential race]. Both Barack Obama and John McCain are gung ho for expanding AmeriCorps to hire a quarter million people to perform federally orchestrated good deeds. Former presidential candidate Senator Chris Dodd wanted to make community service mandatory for high school students and boost AmeriCorps to a million members. John Edwards also favored making national service mandatory.

But does America have a shortage of government workers?

Putting a Smiley Face on Uncle Sam

AmeriCorps is the epitome of contemporary federal good intentions. AmeriCorps, which currently has roughly 75,000 paid recruits, has been very popular in Washington in part because it puts a smiley face on Uncle Sam at a time when many government policies are deeply unpopular.

AmeriCorps has consumed more than $4 billion in tax dollars since its creation in 1993. During the [Bill] Clinton administration, AmeriCorps members helped run a program in Buffalo that gave children $5 for each toy gun they brought in—as well as a certificate praising their decision not to play with toy guns. In San Diego, AmeriCorps members busied themselves collecting used bras and panties for a homeless shelter. In Los Angeles, AmeriCorps members busied themselves foisting unreliable ultra-low-flush toilets on poor people. In New Jersey, AmeriCorps members enticed middle-class families to accept subsidized federal health insurance for their children.

President George W. Bush was a vigorous supporter of AmeriCorps in his 2000 campaign, and many Republicans expected that his team would make the program a pride to the nation. But the program is still an administrative train wreck. In 2002, it illegally spent more than $64 million than Congress appropriated—and yet was rewarded with a higher budget.

Bush's first AmeriCorps chief, Leslie Lenkowsky, started out as a visionary idealist who promised great things from the federal program. But, when he resigned in 2003, Lenkowsky conceded that AmeriCorps is just "another cumbersome, unpredictable government bureaucracy."

No Credible Evidence

Though AmeriCorps abounds in "feel-good" projects, it has never provided credible evidence of benefit to the United States. Instead, it relies on Soviet bloc-style accounting—merely counting labor inputs and pretending that the raw numbers prove grandiose achievements. The Office of Management and Budget concluded in 2003 that "AmeriCorps has not been able to demonstrate results. Its current focus is on the amount of time a person serves, as opposed to the impact on the community or participants." The General Accounting Office [GAO] noted that AmeriCorps "generally reports the results of its programs and activities by quantifying the amount of services AmeriCorps participants perform." GAO criticized AmeriCorps for failing to make any effort to measure the actual effect of its members' actions.

Most AmeriCorps success claims have no more credibility than a political campaign speech. The vast majority of AmeriCorps programs are "self evaluated": The only evidence AmeriCorps possesses of what a program achieved is what the grant recipients claim. One of the agency's consultants encouraged AmeriCorps programs to inflate the number of claimed beneficiaries: "If you feel your program affects a broad group of individuals who may not be receiving personal services from members . . . then list the whole community."

The advocates of a vast national service program assume that there are legions of unmet needs that the new government workers could perform. But the reason such needs are currently unmet is that politicians have either considered them not part of government's obligation or because meeting the need is not considered worth the cost to taxpayers. There are hundreds of thousands of government agencies across the land, counting federal, state, and local governments. There are already more than 20 million people working for government in this country. Yet national service advocates talk as if the public sector is starved of resources.

More Profitable for Politicians than for Citizens

National service programs are more profitable for politicians than for citizens. *USA Today* noted in 1998 that AmeriCorps's "T-shirted brigade is most well known nationally as the youthful backdrop for White House photo ops." President Bush politically exploited AmeriCorps members almost as often as did Clinton.

Some congressmen also profiteer off AmeriCorps's image. After some congressmen showed up one day in March 2004 to hammer some nails at a Habitat for Humanity house-building project in Washington, AmeriCorps issued a press release hyping their participation in the good deed. The press release named eight members of Congress and noted, "Working alongside the elected officials were two dozen AmeriCorps members from the D.C. chapter of Habitat for Humanity and AmeriCorps." The home they helped build was to be given to a single mother of three. Photos from the appearance could add flourishes to newsletters to constituents or for reelection campaigns. Congressmen also benefit when they announce AmeriCorps grants to organizations in their districts.

Some national service advocates insist that AmeriCorps's failings should not be held against proposals to expand the federal role in service because their preferred program would leave it up to communities to decide how to use the new "volunteers."

But if programs are not centrally controlled, local "initiatives" will soon transform it into a national laughingstock. This happened with CETA [the Comprehensive Employment and Training Act], a make-work program that was expanded to its doom under President [Jimmy] Carter. CETA bankrolled such job-creating activities as building an artificial rock in Oregon for rock climbers to practice on, conducting a nude sculpture class in Miami where aspiring artists practiced Braille reading on each other, and sending CETA workers door-to-door in Florida to recruit people for food stamps.

More than 60 million Americans work as unpaid volunteers each year. Even if AmeriCorps was expanded to a quarter million recruits, it would amount to less than one-half of one percent of the total of people who donate their time for what they consider good causes. And there is no reason to assume that paying "volunteers" multiplies productivity.

Rather than expanding national service programs, Congress should pull the plug on AmeriCorps. At a time of soaring deficits, the federal government can no longer afford to spend half a billion dollars a year on a bogus volunteer program whose results have been AWOL since the last century.

Periodical Bibliography

The following articles have been selected to supplement the diverse views presented in this chapter.

American Interest	"A Call to National Service," January 2008.
Jeffrey Anderson	"Safety at Risk for Peace Corps Volunteers," *Washington Times*, June 17, 2010.
Atlantic Monthly	"The Least We Can Do," October 2010.
Pablo Eisenberg	"Why We Might Not Need a Public-Service Academy," *Chronicle of Philanthropy*, January 29, 2009.
Michael Honda and Thomas Petri	"Want a Better, Safer World? Volunteer," *Christian Science Monitor*, March 6, 2009.
Holly La Fon	"Voluntourism: Seeing and Serving the World," *Success*, July 2009.
Mark Neumann	"Volunteerism in Vogue," *Baltimore Jewish Times*, February 13, 2009.
Beth Douglass Silcox	"At Our Service: Teaching Kids to Lead the Way and Give as They Go," *Success*, November 2009.
Richard Stengel	"A Time to Serve," *Time*, August 30, 2007.
Pearl Stewart	"You Can Work as a Volunteer: Want to Make a Difference? Volunteer!" *Black Collegian*, September 2009.

What Is the Social Impact of National Service?

Chapter Preface

Studies show that national service cultivates an ethic of service. This social impact of service is one reason advocates claim that support of national service programs should continue. In *Still Serving: Measuring the Eight-Year Impact of AmeriCorps on Alumni*,[1] the authors found that those who serve continue to do so long after their initial service commitment is completed. According to the study, 60 percent of AmeriCorps state and national alumni work in a nonprofit or governmental organization to solve their communities' pressing needs after their service commitment is completed. While few dispute this result, the study also shows that this effect is not long lived. Moreover, some assert, these results may be influenced by the fact that those who choose national service are already actively engaged in their communities. Still others claim that government-sponsored national service actually threatens true volunteerism.

The *Still Serving* study of the impact of AmeriCorps on alumni demonstrates many positive, lasting effects on those who serve. Eight years after service, those who participated in the study continued to be civically engaged. Indeed, 69 percent of AmeriCorps alumni participate in community meetings and activities. The study also reveals that 46 percent of those studied pursued careers in education, social work, public safety, and government or military service. This impact appears to be even more pronounced among disadvantaged alumni, who are more likely to be employed in public service careers. The report's authors conclude, "AmeriCorps members gain a sense of empowerment to continue their participation long after they complete the program."

1. The report, published in May 2008, was coauthored by the Corporation for National and Community Service and the research and consulting firm Abt Associates Inc.

Despite these results, the study authors note that these effects tend to fade over time. While alumni continue to be connected to their communities, the strength of their civic engagement decreases, the study authors maintain. Others caution that those who evaluate these results should acknowledge that those who choose to volunteer might have characteristics that influence the choice to volunteer in the first place, and these characteristics may influence their choice to volunteer once their service is complete. Nevertheless, they assert, this does not diminish the program's benefits. According to Diana Epstein, in her August 2009 doctoral degree dissertation on the impact of national service, "Even though those who choose to participate may already be on a trajectory of higher civic engagement and volunteerism than those who do not participate, it is reasonable to believe that service in AmeriCorps may have an additional added benefit."[2]

Opponents argue that government-sponsored national service does not foster an ethic of service, nor does it teach compassion or responsibility. In fact, they claim, programs such as AmeriCorps actually diminish the meaning of true volunteerism. Moreover, they maintain, it is not the function of government to cultivate personal character. According to Matthew Spalding, a scholar at the Heritage Foundation, a conservative think tank, "government-directed 'volunteerism,' by encouraging individuals and associations to look to the state as the provider of assistance, belittles authentic volunteerism, the process by which individuals choose without economic benefit to help their neighbor."[3] In his view, true civic responsibility is best promoted by encouraging truly voluntary service managed by private organizations. "The better course," Spalding reasons, "is to bolster the call to service by encouraging a true and voluntary citizen service that is consistent with principles

2. Diana Epstein, *Evaluating the Long-Term Impacts of AmeriCorps Service on Participants*, Frederick S. Pardee RAND Graduate School, August 2009.
3. Matthew Spalding, "Compulsory National Service Would Undermine the American Character," *U.S. News & World Report*, October 19, 2010.

of self-government, is harmonious with a vibrant civil society, and promotes a service agenda based on personal responsibility, independent citizenship, and civic volunteerism."

Commentators continue to contest whether national service promotes an ethic of service or devalues true volunteerism. The authors in the following chapter debate other social impacts of national service. Policy makers will pay close attention to these debates when considering whether to support these programs.

"Nearly 61 million Americans now give
their time to help their neighbors."

National Service Improves
American Communities

George W. Bush

In the following viewpoint, excerpted from a speech during his second term as president, George W. Bush claims that millions of Americans answer the call to help their neighbors in communities nationwide. Following the September 11, 2001, terrorist attacks, national service programs have fostered a culture of service that continues to make people's lives better, he maintains. Bush cites the Citizen Corps that helped Hurricane Katrina evacuees settle in Houston, Texas, and the Schools of Hope Literacy Project in Madison, Wisconsin, in which volunteers teach children how to read. The compassion of these national service volunteers reveals the spirit of the American people, he concludes.

As you read, consider the following questions:

1. According to Bush, how did Americans respond to the worst attack on the nation?

2. What did the Bush administration do to empower Americans looking to help?

George W. Bush, "Remarks on Voluntarism," Weekly Compilation of Presidential Documents, September 15, 2008.

3. In Bush's view, what influence in our society ought the government not fear?

It is a joy to be here with members of the armies of compassion. I'm really glad you're here. I appreciate your inspiration to our fellow citizens. I believe you are a constant reminder of the true source of our nation's strength, which is the good hearts and souls of the American people.

We have seen the good hearts of our people over the last week [September 2008] as caring volunteers have helped their fellow citizens through Hurricane Gustav and Tropical Storm Hanna. The Red Cross, which provides a vital role in helping the relief efforts and recovery efforts, has been spending millions of dollars to provide shelter and food for the evacuees and to help with the cleanup efforts. . . .

Answering the Call

I appreciate the fact that those here represent the hundreds of thousands of our citizens who answered the call to love a neighbor like we'd like to be loved ourselves. I appreciate the fact that you and others lift up souls, one person at a time. You strengthen the foundation of our democracy, which is the engagement of our people. I want to thank you for what you do. God bless you and welcome. . . .

In my first Inaugural Address [on January 20, 2001], I challenged all Americans to be citizens—not spectators—responsible citizens, building communities of service and a nation of character.

Eight months later, Americans were tested by the worst attack on our nation. In the midst of chaos and sorrow, Americans responded with the—with characteristic courage and grace. It was a remarkable moment in our country. It really was, when you think about it. Rescue workers wrote their Social Security numbers on their arms and then rushed into buildings. Citizens became members of ambulance teams. And people from all across the country poured into New York City to help.

The terrorists who attacked our country on September the 11th didn't understand our country at all. Evil may crush concrete and twisted steel, but it can never break the spirit of the American people.

In the weeks and months after the attacks, inspiring acts continued to unfold all across the country. I'm sure you heard the stories, just like I did. Men and women of our armed forces accepted dangerous new duties, and a lot of folks stepped forward to volunteer to protect our fellow citizens. But the desire to serve reached far beyond the military. Millions of Americans were—really wanted to help our country recover.

Serving the Nation

And so, to tap into that spirit, I called on every American to spend at least 4,000 hours—or 2 years in the course of a lifetime—to serve our nation through acts of compassion. Some said that's acting—asking a lot for the country, and they were right—and they were right. Two years during a lifetime is a lot to give. But the truth of the matter is, citizens who do give realize that they become enriched just like those folks that they're helping.

To empower Americans looking to help, we launched what's called the USA Freedom Corps. The goal of the USA Freedom Corps was to connect Americans with opportunities to serve our country, to foster a culture of citizenship and responsibility and service. Over the last 6 years, the USA Freedom Corps has met these goals.

One way we helped was to launch a website called volunteer.gov, which is the largest clearinghouse of volunteer opportunities in America. In other words, we used high-tech innovations to be able to channel people's desire to serve in a constructive way.

And so, the government—this government website directs people to private charities or local churches or Habitat for Humanity drives or Meals on Wheels—just opportunities to serve their neighbor. We can't put love in somebody's heart, but we certainly can help somebody channel their love. And that was the purpose of the website.

And you can search by hometown. They tell me that if you get on Crawford, Texas, you'll find that the local Humane Society leaks—seeks volunteer pet groomers, which makes Barney really nervous.

This is just one of 4 million volunteer opportunities on the USA Freedom Corps website. Isn't that interesting? There are 4 million opportunities for somebody who wants to serve to say, "Here's how I can help." And so, I urge our fellow citizens to go to the website and find out if there's not something that'll interest you, something that'll give you a chance to serve something greater than yourself.

The USA Freedom Corps fosters a culture of service by encouraging the private sector to step forward. We've got what we call the Pro Bono Challenge, which is—encourages corporate professionals to donate their services to charities and nonprofits. That makes a lot of sense, doesn't it, to encourage corporate America to not only serve their shareholders, but serve the communities in which they exist.

One really interesting, innovative idea came out of IBM this year. IBM employees will donate millions of hours of service to charities in the U.S., as well as technology projects in developing nations. They tell me that this work would cost $250 million if IBM's devoted employees were charging and not providing for free. I want to thank the CEO of IBM, Sam Palmisano, who is with us today. Sam, thank you very much for coming. And I encourage corporate America to figure out ways that they can serve to make America a better place.

Another key component of USA Freedom Corps is our effort to keep track of Americans' service to others. I mean, it's

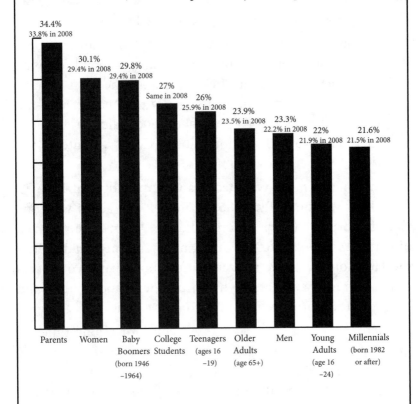

Average National Volunteer Rates

In 2009, 63.4 million Americans volunteered to help their communities, providing 8.1 billion hours of service worth an estimated dollar value of almost $169 billion (dollar value provided by the Independent Sector).

34.4%
33.8% in 2008

30.1%
29.4% in 2008

29.8%
29.4% in 2008

27%
Same in 2008

26%
25.9% in 2008

23.9%
23.5% in 2008

23.3%
22.2% in 2008

22%
21.9% in 2008

21.6%
21.5% in 2008

Parents | Women | Baby Boomers (born 1946 –1964) | College Students | Teenagers (ages 16 –19) | Older Adults (age 65+) | Men | Young Adults (age 16 –24) | Millennials (born 1982 or after)

TAKEN FROM: Corporation for National & Community Service, "2009 Average National Volunteer Rates." www.VolunteeringInAmerica.gov.

one thing to talk about it; it's another thing to measure, to kind of see how we're doing. In 2002, this administration became the first to conduct a regular survey of volunteerism through the U.S. Census Bureau. Because we've brought— begun to measure, we know that nearly 61 million Americans now give their time to help their neighbors. Isn't that interesting? Sixty-one million of our fellow citizens volunteer.

Helping Those Who Want to Serve

We've also launched new national programs and enhanced others to help our citizens answer the call to service. For example, we helped Americans answer the call by creating the Citizen Corps. . . . And we are glad you're here.

For those of you who don't know what the Citizen Corps is, it's a way for people to volunteer to help respond to disasters. This was set up right after September the 11th. Americans have formed community emergency response teams—fire corps, medical reserve corps, neighborhood watch groups. Today, there are nearly 1 million Citizen Corps volunteers nationwide.

And one of those volunteers is County Judge Ed Emmett from Harris County, Texas. So, let me tell you about what the Citizen Corps of Harris County did. So, [Hurricane] Katrina hits, there's about 200,000 Gulf Coast residents headed into the Houston area. The Citizen Corps showed up. Volunteers came to process evacuees, to help treat the ill and injured, and to help settle storm victims in permanent housing.

Here's what Ed said—I've known him for a long time, by the way—the Judge said: "That's just what members of the Citizen Corps do; they take care of their neighbors." And Judge, I want to thank you, and all of the members of the Citizen Corps nationwide for taking care of your neighbors.

Giving Professionals Opportunities to Serve

We've helped Americans answer the call by creating a program called Volunteers for Prosperity. This initiative matched skilled American professionals with service opportunities, a lot of them in the developing world. This year, we mobilized more than 43,000 doctors, teachers, engineers, and other skilled volunteers. That's a pretty good start for an important program, it seems like to me. These men and women save babies from malaria on the continent of Africa. They bring modern information technology to Afghanistan. They live out one of America's strongest beliefs, that to whom much is given, much is required.

One of those people who is a member of this important team is Zach Harvey. He serves on the prosthetics staff at Walter Reed Army Medical Center. . . . When he isn't busy helping our wounded warriors, he's putting his skills to use in Guatemala and the Dominican Republic as a Volunteer for Prosperity. He works with pediatric cancer patients who've had a limb amputated as part of their treatment. He and his team of volunteers fit the children with new limbs, and they pass on their skills to other caregivers.

He says the only payment he receives is the pride that comes with children's—seeing children walk again. And Zach, we are proud to have you here, and thank you for your service. Zach doesn't want anybody to look at him . . . but you can't help it when you're that kind of kind man. Appreciate it.

By the way, both the Citizen Corps and Volunteers for Prosperity have been very effective programs. And I really believe Congress needs to make these good programs permanent.

Strengthening AmeriCorps

We've also helped answer the call to service by strengthening AmeriCorps. This is a program that matches dedicated volunteers with hundreds of private charitable institutions. AmeriCorps members sign up for 1-year commitments with the idea of strengthening their communities by teaching adults how to read or improving health care or helping the homeless put a roof over their heads. This is a good program that was started by my predecessor, President [Bill] Clinton.

After 9/11, we tried to make this program more effective, in other words, to help the dollars allocated go further. Today, more than 74,000 people serve their fellow citizens through AmeriCorps. I have met AmeriCorps volunteers all over our country, and they're very inspiring Americans.

One such volunteer was—is Emily Greene. After college, she enlisted in the program to serve with the Schools of Hope Literacy Project in Madison, Wisconsin. Through the Schools of Hope, Emily has recruited hundreds of volunteers to teach children how to read. What kind of—what a wonderful gift. When somebody says, "How can I help serve America?," how about teaching a child to read as a lasting contribution to the future of our country.

Madison's public elementary schools are improving; the achievement gap is narrowing. And Emily, it must make you feel great to leave a lasting contribution. And we are glad you're here on behalf of AmeriCorps. Thanks for coming.

Expanding the Peace Corps

We've also helped others serve by expanding the Peace Corps. So, see, you don't know what I know: That every time I go to an embassy overseas and I mention anything about the Peace Corps, and there happens to be a Peace Corps contingent— they give that same kind of yell. Peace Corps volunteers are incredibly motivated people, and it's a fabulous program.

The number of Peace Corps volunteers has increased. We've reopened 13—reopened programs in 13 countries. This is a vital program. There are about 8,000 Peace Corps members. They are fighting AIDS in Africa, training poor workers to start their own businesses in Latin America; they're teaching English to children in Asia. What they're doing is they're showing the rest of the world the compassionate heart of the American citizens. I mean, we are a compassionate nation, and the Peace Corps does a fabulous job of advancing that compassion.

Praya Baruch is with us today. After college, Praya spent 2 years in Ghana working with people who are HIV positive, training religious leaders to provide community-based care, and educating young people about HIV [prevention]. She is now on the staff of the Peace Corps. She represents the 8,000 people who are on the front lines of helping people deal with some of the more—most difficult problems in the world. Praya, we are honored you're here, and I want to thank the Peace Corps.

There are other ways to help Americans answer the call to service. We have got what we call the Faith-Based and Community Initiative through which we've empowered Americans to volunteer through their churches and congregations.

Welcoming the Influence of Faith

You know, I believe that if a program is successful, government ought to support it. And I believe if it takes faith to help some—solve some of the most intractable problems, government ought not to fear the influence of faith in our society, we ought to welcome the influence of faith in our society.

Laura—who is not here, but sends her best wishes—has rallied thousands of volunteers to help at-risk children through Helping America's Youth Initiative. We've encouraged volunteerism by holding up examples of our volunteers. You know, to date, 1.1 million Americans have received the President's Volunteer Service Award. That may not seem like a big deal to some people, but when you get one and you show it to people you're working with, they say, "How do I get one of those?" "What do I need to do?" Well, what you need to do is serve your community by volunteering and help make somebody's life better.

Volunteerism is strong in the country. But the truth of the matter is, the farther we've gotten away from 9/11, that memory has begun to fade. And some are saying, "Well, maybe I don't need to volunteer now. Maybe the crisis has passed." The aftermath of 9/11 isn't nearly as intense as it was. And my call to people is, there's always a need. You should be volunteering not because of 9/11, but you should be volunteering because our country needs you on a regular basis.

We can use your help. There are citizens who say, "I need love." Government can pass law, but it cannot put love into somebody's heart. Oftentimes that helps when somebody puts their arm around you and says, "How can I help you, brother or sister? What can I do to make your life better?"

Renewing the Call

And so, today I call upon our fellow citizens to devote 4,000 hours over your lifetime in service to your country. You'll become a better person for it, and our society will be more healthy as a result of it. You know, there's an old adage that says, you can bring hope to the lives of others, but the life you enrich the most will probably be your own.

I've witnessed the amazing phenomena of volunteerism throughout my travels in this country. At nearly every stop, I make it a point to meet a local volunteer selected by the USA Freedom Corps at the steps of Air Force One. After they get over the initial shock of seeing me come off the plane—I love to ask them what they're doing; what are you doing to make your community a better place?

One such volunteer is a young woman I met in Pittsburgh named Kristen Holloway. She started a program called Operation Troop Appreciation. It started off as kind of a small program, just an idea, a desire to make a statement. Her group collects everything from DVDs and phone calls—cards to musical instruments and sports gear. So far, they have sent care packages to more than 40,000 men and women serving on the front lines in this war against the extremists. . . .

Kristen, we're glad you're here. Thank you for—by the way, you're representing a lot of people here in this audience and around the country who have had—have had the honor of meeting as volunteers at the foot of Air Force One.

Inspiring Volunteers

I want to thank you all for showing up when I show up. Generally, the weather is nice; sometimes it's not so nice. But nevertheless, you're there with your smiling face, and you inspire me. You really do lift up my spirits, to meet people who are so dedicated that they are willing to take time out of their lives to help somebody in need. And I hope by getting you on the front page of your newspapers, that you inspire others to show up and serve America by volunteering.

But I want to tell you what the—what a soldier wrote to Kristen's group. A soldier wrote back after getting one of the packages and said, "My heart soars with pride to represent a country filled with such wonderful people as you." That was the thank-you note that Kristen's group got.

Well, my heart soars with pride as well to be in the presence of those who are lifting up souls and helping mend hearts. I want to thank you for what you're doing. I am incredibly optimistic about the future of our county. And the reason I am is because I've seen firsthand the love and the compassion and the decency of our fellow citizens.

May God bless you. May God bless the armies of compassion.

> "AmeriCorps has not been able to demonstrate results. Its current focus is on the amount of time a person serves, as opposed to the impact on the community."

National Service Has Little Impact on American Communities

James Bovard

James Bovard, who writes about threats to individual freedom in books such as Freedom in Chains, *argues in the following viewpoint that national service has little impact on communities. In fact, he maintains, national service programs simply give politicians an opportunity to flaunt their goodness. Bovard points to AmeriCorps programs that he claims are more sanctimonious than useful. Although national programs such as AmeriCorps have never proven that they do any good, laws to expand these programs continue to ask citizens to offer their time or their tax dollars to serve the moral values of their leaders.*

James Bovard, "National Disservice," *American Conservative*, April–May 6, 2009, pp. 20–22. Reproduced by permission.

As you read, consider the following questions:

1. In Bovard's opinion, by how much does the GIVE Act increase the number of slots for AmeriCorps members?

2. What does the author claim is presented as a prime justification for increasing the size of AmeriCorps?

3. In the author's view, what model of virtue is the claim that AmeriCorps members mobilize 1.7 million other Americans to volunteer?

On March 18, [2009] the House of Representatives voted 321-105 to pass the Generations Invigorating Volunteerism and Education Act [later renamed the Edward M. Kennedy Serve America Act], and the Senate is expected quickly to follow suit. The GIVE Act more than triples the number of slots for AmeriCorps members from 75,000 to 250,000. And it takes a giant step toward expanding Washington's power to make "service" compulsory for all young Americans.

President [Barack] Obama praises AmeriCorps for embodying "the best of our nation's history, diversity and commitment to service." In reality, AmeriCorps's essence is paying people on false pretenses to do unnecessary things.

Since President [Bill] Clinton created the program in 1993, politicians of both parties have endlessly touted its recruits as volunteers toiling selflessly for the common good. But the average AmeriCorps member receives more than $15,000 a year in pay and other benefits, and almost 90 percent go on to work for government agencies or nonprofit groups. Rather than financial martyrdom, signing up for AmeriCorps is, for many, akin to a paid internship.

A Laughingstock

Even though AmeriCorps is popular with the Washington establishment, it has always been a laughingstock. During the Clinton administration, AmeriCorps members helped run a program in Buffalo that gave children $5 for each toy gun they brought in, as well as a certificate praising their decision not to play with these trinkets. In San Diego, AmeriCorps members busied themselves collecting used bras and panties for a homeless shelter. In Los Angeles, they foisted unreliable ultra-low-flush toilets on poor people.

Indeed, AmeriCorps's projects produce little more than sanctimony and headlines for news-starved local newspapers. Among the program's recent coups:

- In San Francisco, AmeriCorps members busy themselves mediating elementary school playground disputes.

- In Florida, AmeriCorps recruits in the Women in Distress program organized a poetry reading on the evils of domestic violence.

- In Oswego, New York, they set up a donation bin to gather used cell phones for victims of domestic violence.

- In Montana, members encouraged people to donate books to ship to Cameroon.

- In Lafayette, Louisiana, with help from the local Junior League, AmeriCorps led an effort to recycle prom dresses for high school students.

And 11 AmeriCorps members spent several weeks at a Biloxi, Mississippi, elementary school last fall [2008] helping the school "go green." Students gathered more than 3,000 pounds of recyclable material. Much was paper, which is currently fetching barely $100 a ton, but the project presumably made all participants glow with virtue.

Puppet shows are a favorite activity for AmeriCorps members around the country. In Springfield, Illinois, they donned puppets to school 3-year-olds at the Little Angels Child Care Center about the benefits of smoke detectors.

Reading-related and other education activities are often presented as a prime justification for tripling the program's size. President Clinton set the standard when he declared in a 1997 radio address touting AmeriCorps's literacy efforts: "All you really need to do is to roll up your sleeves, sit with a child and open a book together." When it comes to the hard work of actually teaching kids how to read, opening books is apparently "close enough for government work." But in truth, AmeriCorps has shown little if any competence at teaching literacy. It makes do with a "fun with books" motif that provides as much benefit as watching a few episodes of *Sesame Street*.

Not a Scandal-Free History

Newsweek editor Jonathan Alter, one of the program's biggest proponents, praises AmeriCorps for its "15 years of scandal-free" history. Not exactly.

The program was tainted from the get-go. In its early years, members were routinely used as backdrops for photo opportunities when President Clinton arrived on tarmacs around the nation. And AmeriCorps "volunteers" were repeatedly involved in political advocacy and petitioning. The program gave over $1 million to ACORN [Association of Community Organizations for Reform Now].

The Mississippi Action for Community Education [MACE] AmeriCorps program was purportedly recruiting food stamp recipients. In reality, it was stacking the payroll with ghost employees. MACE's director was convicted on 15 felony counts and sent to prison in 2002. And last year, Sacramento's St. HOPE [Leadership] Academy, a showcase AmeriCorps program, was disbarred after an inspector-general investigation found that AmeriCorps members were detailed to serve as personal assistants to the academy's founder, to perform menial work for the academy, and "to engage in political campaigning to the benefit of St. HOPE's charter school."

But AmeriCorps remains popular on Capitol Hill, at least in part because it allows members of Congress to flaunt their goodness. The program's headquarters encourages local branches to organize "AmeriCorps-for-a-Day events with elected officials" to help get them on board. After some pols [politicians] showed up one day five years ago to hammer a few nails at a D.C. house-building project, AmeriCorps issued a press release naming and praising the eight members of Congress. Photos from appearances at AmeriCorps Habitat for Humanity projects can embellish constituent newsletters and aid in re-election campaigns.

Exploiting AmeriCorps

Politicians exploit AmeriCorps in other ways. Early in his first term, President George W. Bush hyped the expansion of AmeriCorps as a counterpunch against Osama bin Laden. Shortly after 9/11 [referring to the terrorist attacks of September 11, 2001], AmeriCorps chief Leslie Lenkowsky told members, "the daily duties that you perform will also be helping to thwart terrorism itself." He assured AmeriCorps recruits that their efforts were "as important to our nation's security and well-being" as the actions of American troops at that moment fighting the Taliban in Afghanistan. By 2003, Lenkowsky changed his tune, describing AmeriCorps as just "another cumbersome, unpredictable government bureaucracy."

AmeriCorps claims that its members "mobilize" 1.7 million other Americans to volunteer each year. At best, this is the Tom Sawyer model of virtue—some people getting paid to sway other people to work for free. AmeriCorps's actual achievements are a statistical charade. The organization routinely counts anyone who works in a project that AmeriCorps members "manage" as a new volunteer. Thus, if 20 people are already working at a house-building project where an AmeriCorps member temporarily supervises, they are all counted as AmeriCorps-generated volunteers.

Ballard Street

Volunteerism is not for the faint of heart.

No Evidence of Result

AmeriCorps trumpets the assertion that, since its creation, "540,000 AmeriCorps members have contributed more than 705 million hours of service." Shirley Sagawa, a Clinton White House official, observed that presidents have always "set the measure of AmeriCorps [as] the number of bodies in it." But

AmeriCorps has never performed a credible analysis of the value of the service its members produce. Instead, it relies on Soviet bloc-style accounting—merely counting labor inputs and pretending the raw numbers prove grandiose achievements.

In 2003, the Office of Management and Budget concluded that "AmeriCorps has not been able to demonstrate results. Its current focus is on the amount of time a person serves, as opposed to the impact on the community or participants." The General Accounting Office criticized the organization for failing to make any effort to measure the actual effect of its members' actions.

But Congress continues to fill AmeriCorps ranks because it puts a smiley face on big government. Whether or not they produce anything, as long as AmeriCorps's gray shirts are out there getting PR [public relations] for helping people, Leviathan [something very large or powerful] can be portrayed as a giant engine of compassion. "National service" is really just any subsidized activity that burnishes the image of the federal government.

The Threat of Compulsory Service

If AmeriCorps were simply a garden-variety boondoggle, the fairy tales about its achievements would be relatively benign (except to taxpayers). But some politicians hope to exploit AmeriCorps's cachet to gin up [enliven] support for imposing compulsory labor requirements on all young Americans.

The GIVE Act calls for the appointment of a Congressional Commission on Civic Service, raising the obvious question of whether congressmen deserve vastly more power over other Americans. But in Washington logic, since volunteering is a good thing, everybody should be forced to do it.

The commission will examine "the effect on the nation . . . if all individuals in the United States . . . were required to perform a certain amount of national service" and "whether a workable, fair, and reasonable mandatory service requirement for all able young people could be developed." It will also consider whether tacitly repealing the 13th Amendment prohibition on involuntary servitude "would strengthen the social fabric of the Nation and overcome civic challenges by bringing together people from diverse economic, ethnic, and educational backgrounds."

Would political subjugation produce moral uplift? The Beltway [Washington, DC] answer of course—because politicians are the nation's leaders, the de facto "best and brightest." While they are destroying the nation's financial future with one trillion-dollar bailout after another, they have the gall to lecture young people about their obligations to the government.

The GIVE Act views military-style regimentation as a model for the nation. Its National Civil Community Corps would seek to "combine the best practices of civilian service with the best aspects of military service." This reminds some critics of Obama's declaration last July: "We've got to have a civilian national security force that is just as powerful, just as strong, just as well funded as the military."

This is in character with Obama's liberalism. Shortly after his election victory last November, the change.gov website announced the new president's call for "developing a plan to require 50 hours of community service in middle school and high school and 100 hours of community service in college every year." The wording was later changed to "setting a goal" for service. (Some states have already imposed such requirements on students as a condition for graduation.)

This is part of a long series of Democratic Party efforts to create pretexts to commandeer more of people's lives. A dozen years ago, in a stunning conflation of compassion and compulsion, President Clinton announced that America needs "citizen servants." He declared, "The will to serve has never been stronger." That may or may not have been true, but the will to power is certainly at a high-water mark.

A *New York Times* editorial on March 24 hailed the GIVE Act for providing "a chance to constructively harness the idealism of thousands of Americans eager to contribute time and energy to solving the nation's problems." But the GIVE Act is idealistic only if one believes that citizens should take their values—and their "moral opportunities"—from their rulers.

It is a sad day when people line up to have their virtue certified by the most exploitative, dishonest class in the nation.

"[Benjamin Franklin] emphasized deeds over words. He was also for supporting any faith that forged good works."

National Service Transcends Religious and Secular Differences

John J. DiIulio

John J. DiIulio maintains in the following viewpoint that national service is about doing good deeds and therefore transcends religious and secular differences. For example, he claims, the University of Pennsylvania, a secular university, made a five-year commitment to service learning in hurricane-ravaged New Orleans through internships sponsored by Catholic Charities. The covenant to serve, DiIulio argues, is not between secular and religious partners but between those who serve and the people whose lives they are helping reclaim. DiIulio, a political science professor at the University of Pennsylvania, served as director of the White House Office of Faith-Based and Community Initiatives in 2001.

John J. DiIulio, "A Covenant to Serve," *America*, March 23, 2009, p. 10. Reproduced by permission of America Press. For subscription information, visit www.americamagazine .org.

As you read, consider the following questions:

1. What does DiIulio view as a shameful failure following Hurricane Katrina?

2. How, according to the author, do Hispanic immigrants continue to be exploited in New Orleans?

3. How many weeks of service have University of Pennsylvania undergraduates and graduates dedicated to New Orleans since September 2005?

As I write this [2009], I am two weeks away from making my 14th trip to post-Hurricane Katrina New Orleans. I am reflecting on how in late August 2005, four-fifths of that city was flooded when three poorly built levees broke beneath Katrina's blows. The resulting death and devastation made grim headlines worldwide.

So did official Washington's shameful, almost surreal failure to rush resources to the rescue. The disaster's predominantly African-American, low-income victims were not treated as fellow citizens. Some politicians and journalists even took to calling these suddenly homeless Americans "refugees."

Were it not for heroics by the U.S. Coast Guard, Katrina's initial human, property and financial toll would have been much worse. And were it not for nonprofit organizations, ranging from little local congregations to citywide operations like Catholic Charities of New Orleans, the post-Katrina recovery process would have moved even slower.

Ills Remain in New Orleans

It has been three-and-a-half years since biblical-sized floods blanketed the Big Easy [a nickname for New Orleans]. Poverty, crime and other ills that were bad before are bad or worse there today. Affordable housing, health care and other basic human needs are far from well met. Many Hispanic im-

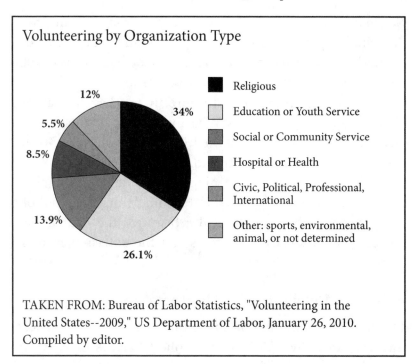

Volunteering by Organization Type

12%

34% — Religious

5.5%

Education or Youth Service

8.5%

Social or Community Service

Hospital or Health

13.9%

Civic, Political, Professional, International

Other: sports, environmental, animal, or not determined

26.1%

TAKEN FROM: Bureau of Labor Statistics, "Volunteering in the United States--2009," US Department of Labor, January 26, 2010. Compiled by editor.

migrants involved in hazardous cleanup or construction jobs continue to be exploited by unscrupulous employers.

Still, New Orleans now has about three-fourths of its pre-Katrina population. Even in these bad financial times, its economy is jazzy and growing. Its natives' infectiously warm hospitality and inimitable civic spirit have been revived. Its struggling Hispanic residents have given the historic city's de-mographic gumbo its first mighty 21st-century stirring. Volunteer-saints from all across the United States still go marching in to help.

As on my previous post-Katrina trips, I will not be alone. Over 100 spring break student-volunteers from the University of Pennsylvania will be with me. Though Penn is a proudly nonsectarian Ivy League university, founded by Benjamin Franklin, it boasts undergraduate student religious life organi-zations that make for a marvelous faith-based mosaic: Jewish students with the Hillel Center, Catholic students with the

Newman Center and over a dozen other groups. I am proud that since September 2005, these groups and other Penn undergraduates and recent graduates have dedicated over 1,000 weeks of service in post-Katrina New Orleans.

But my Penn pride here also directly touches my Catholic identity. Speaking at Penn's Wharton School of Business on Oct. 14, 2005, Archbishop Alfred C. Hughes of New Orleans energized the predominantly non-Catholic crowd by telling how the archdiocese was opening its arms and its schools to poor children of every faith and of no faith. Non-Catholic colleagues who have never held a brief for the church were moved (in several cases to tears) by the soft-spoken archbishop.

A Secular-Religious Civic Partnership

Thereafter, in communications with me and other Penn colleagues, Jim Kelly, C.E.O. of Catholic Charities of New Orleans, laid down a civic marker: If Penn would make a five-year commitment to service learning in the city, Catholic Charities would cosponsor internships and other initiatives with Penn there.

An elite secular university located 1,100 miles away working in tandem with a Catholic nonprofit? Kelly termed the improbable secular-religious civic partnership "a covenant to serve." . . .

As Kelly has so eloquently stated, the covenant is not between secular Penn and its Catholic partners, but between both of them and the people whose lives were shattered and shuttered by the floods, people who now seek to rebuild their city and reclaim their communities.

The covenant continues. Starting this summer, five recent Penn graduates will be working full time in New Orleans on various Catholic Charities community-serving projects.

Maybe the partnership is not so improbable after all. Franklin started Philadelphia's first library company, giving it a

Latin motto that translates thus: "To pour forth benefits for the common good is divine." Penn's founder emphasized deeds over words. He was also for supporting any faith that forged good works.

Sound familiar?

| "The thousands of student, faith-based and other volunteers who still flock to the city to gut and rebuild houses actually contribute to the . . . dismantling [of] the public sphere."

Some National Service Programs Displace the Poor

Sara Falconer

In the following viewpoint, journalist Sara Falconer maintains that some national service efforts do more to displace the poor than help them. She points, for example, to rebuilding in New Orleans following Hurricane Katrina. The poorest residents are being abandoned and public housing is being destroyed while volunteers build private homes that many cannot afford, Falconer argues. To counter the deliberate displacement of the poor in communities such as New Orleans, a different kind of volunteerism is needed—support in the fight for the rights of those who need public housing and public services, she concludes.

As you read, consider the following questions:

1. Why, in Falconer's opinion, do many citizens of New Orleans have no incentive to return to their communities?

Sara Falconer, "Saints or Scabs? The Impact of Volunteer Labour in New Orleans," *Briarpatch*, November–December 2009. Reproduced by permission.

2. How many people does the author claim have been displaced from New Orleans and sought work in other cities?

3. In the author's view, what must replace charity as a mantra to help the poorest residents of New Orleans?

It's not easy getting a cab to the Lower Ninth Ward [in New Orleans, Louisiana]. Even now, with most of the former population cleared out, some drivers still won't cross the Claiborne Avenue Bridge unless it's to take a carload of tourists to gawk at Hurricane Katrina's Ground Zero. So when the third cab stops, it's with some impatience that I ask if he knows the way.

"Oh sure, sweetie," he drawls. "Born and raised. Born and raised."

Norman is a retired firefighter who now drives cab to supplement his pension. Four years ago, after Hurricane Katrina [2005], he patrolled the flooded streets by boat to pull survivors from rooftops and attic windows. When he learns that my companion and I have travelled from Toronto to volunteer with a grassroots rebuilding project called Common Ground Relief, chatty Norman gets very quiet. He reaches over, turns off the meter and looks at us intently. "I want to show you something," he says.

Although it's late, he drives several blocks past our destination, his headlights occasionally framing the sagging ruin of a house or an exposed foundation, the structure either washed away or bulldozed by the city. He distractedly points out the levees where the water first broke through, just steps from these front doors. Finally he stops at a cheery bungalow, its porch light blazing, a tidy little oasis of normalcy in the darkness.

"This is my home," Norman says, his gruff voice choked with emotion. "Volunteers rebuilt it for me."

He hopes his return will encourage his neighbours to come back too, but there is much that stands in their way. With their homes and jobs long gone, we wonder, what incentive is there for anyone to return? And how much of a difference can small groups of parachuted-in volunteers make when there is such substantial work to be done?

A Part of the Problem

The jarring reality, we will soon discover, is that volunteers like us are, unwittingly, at least as much a part of the problem as a part of the solution. Real change in New Orleans—the kind that will give the rest of Norman's community a reason to return—is going to require solidarity of an entirely different kind. It's not the "thousand points of light" feel-good charity work that [President George H.W.] Bush championed. Rather, it's the rebirth of a civil rights-era approach that put thousands of activists on the front lines of struggles, in direct confrontation with the State.

Since 2005, much of the city has been rebuilt, particularly in the wealthy Garden District and French Quarter. The Lower Ninth Ward, though, remains a wasteland. Of the 19,000 people who lived there when Katrina hit, only 3,600 have come back. Many of the rest have been mired in red tape trying to access insurance or relief funds for so long that they can no longer afford the trip home. The city seems to actively discourage resettlement, routinely levying large fines against absent homeowners for infractions such as excessive grass length, eventually going so far as to expropriate and demolish the offending homes.

Intentional Displacement

The intentional displacement of low-income communities from this area is nothing new, says Jay Arena, a longtime activist in the fight to defend public housing in New Orleans, both before and after Katrina. "The city had wiped out half of the public housing even before the storm," he explains, from 14,000 to 7,000 units during the 1990s and early 2000s. In 2008, under the guidance of the [George W.] Bush administration, the Housing Authority of New Orleans (HANO) destroyed another 5,000 low-income apartments. Charity Hospital, providing care to tens of thousands of uninsured, was also shut down—all part of a push to replace public services with for-profit ventures.

"It's about dismantling the public sector and letting charity groups address the ensuing social ills," Arena fumes. "That has been the neoliberal agenda of the elite, local and national, post-Katrina."

Arena is critical of the role of nonprofits, foundations and universities in underwriting that agenda. With the U.S. Department of Housing and Urban Development (HUD) poised to destroy public housing (which they label "concentrated poverty" to justify their efforts to eradicate it) across the country, New Orleans became the latest victim of an all-out offensive on the public sphere—political and economic onslaught that swept the Global South [poor, developing nations] in recent decades, under International Monetary Fund-imposed austerity measures, and that is now coming home to roost in the Empire's backyard.

A Privatized Model

As Naomi Klein reports in *The Shock Doctrine*, only days after the hurricane struck, the Heritage Foundation, a prominent right-wing think tank, released recommendations for rebuilding the city on a privatized model. Among 32 changes that were quickly implemented by the Bush administration, the foundation urged a disinvestment in the public school system. Vouchers are now issued by lottery to allow a limited number of low-income children to enroll in private school, leaving other students on waiting lists or simply languishing in underfunded public schools.

Meanwhile, thousands of families who used to live in public housing now live in privately owned apartments, paying more than 30 per cent of their income towards the rent and utilities that HANO's "Section 8" vouchers fail to cover. "These were plans they had already drawn up," Jordan Flaherty, a former union organizer and editor of *Left Turn* magazine, tells *Briarpatch*. "The storm was their opportunity."

An Attack on Black Political Power

"What happened with Katrina is not just an attack on poor folks, but also an attack on black political power in the city," he says. "Pre-Katrina, the teachers' union was the largest and most influential in the city, and a source of middle-class black political power. After Katrina, everyone who worked in the school system, from janitors to teachers, was fired, and the union contract was cancelled."

That shift in political power has also been evident in the changing demographics and political representation of the city, as the majority black city council was slowly replaced by a majority white council.

Arena suggests that despite the best of intentions, the thousands of student, faith-based and other volunteers who still flock to the city to gut and rebuild houses actually contribute to the neoliberal project of dismantling the public sphere. "We have Habitat for Humanity building a few private houses, while thousands of public homes are being destroyed," he points out.

Similarly, Teach for America volunteers were brought in to fill the positions of unionized teachers who were fired, while volunteer health clinics now care for some of the thousands of patients abandoned by the closing of Charity Hospital. Describing the same trend in her native India, Arundhati Roy has called this phenomenon the "NGO-ization of politics": "[Nongovernmental organizations'] *real* contribution is that they defuse political anger and dole out as aid or benevolence what people ought to have by right" (*Public Power in the Age of Empire*, 2004).

A Form of Scabbing

Such volunteerism, Arena points out, is also a form of scabbing that drives down wages for workers. "These are jobs that could be performed by Katrina survivors who desperately need them," he says. Louisiana's unemployment rate, at six per cent, is still the lowest in the country, but is rising quickly, with 15,700 jobs cut in the last year as the recession began to take its toll on the state. Despite the potential jobs that construction could offer, most new houses are prefabricated out of state and shipped in, using local labour for only a few days at a time.

Meanwhile, the over 130,000 people who were displaced from New Orleans have had to seek work in other cities, particularly Baton Rouge [Louisiana], Gulfport-Biloxi [Mississippi], Mobile [Alabama] and Jackson [Mississippi]. Many of these workers abandoned their skilled professions to work as cab drivers, short-order cooks and other low-paid positions. The "right of return" movement championed by grassroots community groups like C3/Hands off Iberville, with which Arena was previously involved, advocates the creation of jobs and the repair and expansion of public infrastructure to enable the displaced to come home.

Arena believes that some developers have been "icing out" black workers from what little construction is actually taking place, pitting migrant Latino workers against black locals. C3/Hands Off Iberville is demanding the enforcement of Section 3 of the 1968 Housing Act, which stipulates that on HUD-funded construction work, at least 30 per cent of jobs must go to local workers. "This is by no means an anti-immigration campaign," he says. "We've been fighting for a public works plan that would be open to all—documented, undocumented. There's plenty of work to be done."

The New Orleans Workers' Center for Racial Justice (NOWCRJ), an advocacy group formed in the aftermath of Katrina, echoes Arena's concern that black workers were "locked out" of the rebuilding process while immigrant workers were "locked in" by companies that falsely promised them security and permanent status for their sacrifices. NOWCRJ aims to organize across race and industry lines to build political power, encouraging the inclusion of labourers, guest workers and homeless residents in campaigns against international human labour trafficking, for the protection of day labourers engaging in dangerous work, and more.

A Need for Movement-Based Volunteerism

Both Arena and Flaherty agree that such movement-based volunteerism, rooted in the civil rights tradition, is key to the solution. It is true solidarity, rather than the "thousand points of light" variety of volunteerism, that is needed, Arena says. "In the midst of this whole assault, we've had more than a million people come to the city [to volunteer]. We would have preferred to see people come down and support the struggles for public housing and public services."

A failed attempt by the AFL-CIO [American Federation of Labor/Congress of Industrial Organizations] to unionize hospitality workers several years before Katrina demonstrates the importance of taking cues from local leadership in establishing such solidarity, Flaherty adds. "If you're not doing something with the guidance of those most affected, it simply won't work."

Make no mistake: Volunteers are needed in New Orleans. Its poorest residents—and some of the most vibrant, warm and strong people you will ever meet—have been abandoned by a city and a society that is being deliberately rebuilt without them. But misguided efforts to help only mask the sources of their suffering. With "solidarity, not charity" as a mantra, there is an opportunity for visitors who really want to make a difference to lend their time and skills to support grassroots groups that are taking a stand against a system of exploitation.

| "[National service] proposals . . . target students and young citizens who aren't wealthy."

National Service Unfairly Targets Poor Young People

Paul Thornton

The call for universal national service is simply another way for wealthy middle-aged people to exploit the young, claims Paul Thornton in the following viewpoint. In addition to questioning how national service can be universal without being mandatory, Thornton also argues that proponents have not adequately explained why young people should be put to work other than simply because they are young. More disturbing, Thornton asserts, is that national service programs target young people who are not wealthy with carrots too small to encourage rich young volunteers. Thornton is an editorial researcher for the Los Angeles Times.

As you read, consider the following questions:

1. In what historical context does Thornton claim John F. Kennedy's quote, "ask not what your country can do for you—ask what you can do for your country" was delivered?

Paul Thornton, "National Service? No Thanks," *Los Angeles Times*, September 19, 2007. Reproduced by permission.

2. According to the author, how many hours of community service does Senator Chris Dodd want high school students to perform?

3. In the author's opinion, why will calls for universal service fade?

If only John F. Kennedy could have known that his inaugural address call to service in 1961—"ask not what your country can do for you—ask what you can do for your country"—would become the rallying cry for generations of rich, middle-aged men to tell us sub-30 ingrates that we're unpatriotic runts who aren't doing enough.

The Gift That Keeps on Giving

Never mind that Kennedy's seductively quotable phrase was in a larger Cold War context of encouraging Americans to show why we're better than those Commie Soviets; beating up on upwardly mobile twentysomethings is the gift that keeps on giving. Try it yourself: "Young people don't _____ enough." (I'll get you started—vote, work, suffer, go to church, serve in the military. . . .)

This attitude stops being funny, however, when pundits and politicians—especially presidential candidates—start calling for policies based on it. Mix in a free-for-all presidential election (in wartime, no less), and let the Gen Y shaming begin!

The latest example comes in the Sept. 10 [2007] cover story of *Time* magazine. In it, writer Richard Stengel argues that the next president should dramatically expand and remake U.S. national service programs to capitalize on historically high rates of volunteerism. Stengel's national service wouldn't be mandatory, but it would involve Washington spending billions of dollars to induce citizens into programs such as a health corps and service academy. Who would do all this volunteering? Us young 'uns, of course:

It is the simple but compelling idea that devoting a year or more to national service, whether military or civilian, should become a countrywide rite of passage, the common expectation and widespread experience of virtually every young American.

Aside from the logically perplexing call for a national service program that's "universal" without being "mandatory" (I imagine government ads similar to antismoking TV spots that shame non-volunteers into conscription), Stengel and others who support such programs never explain in practical terms just why it is that young folks should be the ones doing the volunteering. Intentional or not, national service proponents rely on the common assumption that youth should be put to work because, well, they're youth!

Involuntary Servitude

Just because Stengel stops short of mandatory service doesn't mean others don't go there. Sen. Chris Dodd (D-Conn.) has made national service the centerpiece of his long-shot presidential bid—and part of his plan wouldn't be optional. Dodd, who volunteered for the Peace Corps when the program was in its infancy, wants to require every student in the U.S. to perform 100 hours of community service before they graduate high school. And he isn't alone—fellow Democrat John Edwards, according to *Time*, wants a similar service requirement for high school grads. Imagine their American utopia: millions of uninspired teenagers ditching homework to perform involuntary servitude. Can't you feel the civic pride?

What proposals like Stengel's, Dodd's and Edwards's have in common is that they target students and young citizens who aren't wealthy. Stengel's financial carrots (he suggests a $5,000 federally funded "baby bond" that would mature to about $19,000 by the time someone is old enough to volunteer) are too small to entice the rich to serve. Foisting service on public high school students is even more sinister.

After all, poor children are far more likely to seek free public education than wealthy ones, and a program such as Dodd's would force students most likely to be at the receiving end of community service into, well, community service.

So are any of these plans likely to happen? The answer is, of course, no. Various calls for universal service—both in California and nationwide—have come and gone, and the most recent round of youth-busying proposals will likely fade with the campaign season. But because it's easy to tell those of us who happen to have been born less than 30 years ago that we should do something for our country, don't expect the verbal shaming to end any election cycle soon. This is at least one area in which we can be grateful for politicians' fickleness.

> *"Research has established a strong relationship between volunteering and health: Those who volunteer have lower mortality rates, greater functional ability, and lower rates of depression later in life."*

National Service Promotes Better Health for Volunteers

Corporation for National and Community Service

Those who volunteer for national or community service are healthier than those who do not, maintains the Corporation for National and Community Service (CNCS) in the following viewpoint. CNCS also asserts that volunteers report greater well-being and are less likely to suffer from depression. Volunteers live longer as well; indeed, those who experience the greatest health benefits from volunteering are older volunteers, CNCS claims. Thus, CNCS reasons, efforts to promote volunteering will benefit not only American communities but also the volunteers themselves. Created in 1993, CNCS connects Americans of all ages and backgrounds with opportunities to give back to their communities and their nation.

"The Health Benefits of Volunteering: A Review of the Recent Research," Corporation for National and Community Service, April 2007.

As you read, consider the following questions:

1. According to CNCS, what is the "volunteering threshold"?

2. What did the longitudinal study Americans' Changing Lives survey find?

3. Why are the findings of the CNCS report particularly relevant today, in the author's view?

Over the past two decades, a growing body of research indicates that volunteering provides not just social benefits, but individual health benefits as well. This research has established a strong relationship between volunteering and health: Those who volunteer have lower mortality rates, greater functional ability, and lower rates of depression later in life than those who do not volunteer. Some key findings from this research, along with an analysis of the relationship between volunteering and incidence of mortality and heart disease at the state level, are presented here. . . .

Looking at Key Findings

Older volunteers are most likely to receive greater health benefits from volunteering.

Research has found that volunteering provides older adults (those age 60 or older) with greater benefits than younger volunteers. These benefits include improved physical and mental health and greater life satisfaction. In addition, while depression may serve as a barrier to volunteer participation in midlife adults, it is a catalyst for volunteering among older adults, who may seek to compensate for role changes and attenuated social relations that occur with aging.

Volunteers must meet a "volunteering threshold" to receive significant health benefits.

When considering the relationship of the frequency of volunteering to improved health benefits, researchers have found that there is a "volunteering threshold" for health benefits. That is to say, volunteers must be engaged in a certain amount of volunteering in order to derive health benefits from the volunteer activities. Once that threshold is met, no additional health benefits are acquired by doing volunteering more. The definition of considerable volunteering has been variously defined by these studies as 1) volunteering with two or more organizations; 2) 100 hours or more of volunteer activities per year; and 3) at least 40 hours of volunteering per year.

Volunteering leads to greater life satisfaction and lower rates of depression.

Evidence indicates that volunteering has a positive effect on social psychological factors, such as a personal sense of purpose and accomplishment, and enhances a person's social networks to buffer stress and reduce disease risk. According to one study, when older adults volunteered in 1986, they experienced lower rates of depression in 1994.

A Cycle of Well-Being

Volunteering and physical well-being are part of a positive reinforcing cycle.

A study of longitudinal data from the Americans' Changing Lives survey found that those who volunteered in 1986 reported higher levels of happiness, life satisfaction, self-esteem, a sense of control over life, and physical health in 1989, while those in 1986 who reported higher levels of happiness, life satisfaction, self-esteem, a sense of control over life, and physical health were more likely to volunteer in 1989.

Evidence suggests the possibility that the best way to prevent poor health in the future, which could be a barrier to volunteering, is to volunteer.

A number of studies demonstrate that those individuals who volunteer at an earlier point experience greater functional

Volunteering and Health

Volunteers agree that volunteering helps them to lead healthier lives.

- 68% of volunteers agree that "volunteering has made me feel physically healthier."

- 89% of volunteers agree that "volunteering has improved my sense of well-being."

- 73% of volunteers agree that "volunteering lowers my stress levels."

- 29% of volunteers who suffer from a chronic condition agree that "volunteering has helped me manage a chronic illness."

- Volunteering appears to correspond to a healthier BMI [body mass index]. 34% of volunteers are considered to have an "average" BMI, compared to 27% of non-volunteers. In addition, a lower proportion of volunteers (31%) were identified as obese when compared to non-volunteers (36%).

UnitedHealthcare and VolunteerMatch, "Volunteering and Your Health: How Giving Back Benefits Everyone," 2010.

ability and better health outcomes later in life, even when the studies control for other factors, such as socioeconomic status and previous illness.

Individuals who volunteer live longer.

Several longitudinal studies have found that those individuals who volunteer during the first wave of the survey have lower mortality rates at the second wave of the survey, even when taking into account such factors as physical health, age, socioeconomic status and gender.

Researchers have also found that when patients with chronic or serious illness volunteer, they receive benefits beyond what can be achieved through medical care.

State volunteer rates are strongly connected with the physical health of the state's population.

Using health and volunteering data from the U.S. Census Bureau and the Centers for Disease Control [and Prevention], we find that states with a high volunteer rate also have lower rates of mortality and incidences of heart disease. When comparing states, a general trend shows that health problems are more prevalent in states where volunteer rates are lowest.

The Implications of Research

Studies of the relationship between volunteering and health demonstrate that there is a significant relationship between volunteering and good health: When older adults volunteer, they not only help their community but also experience better health in later years, whether in terms of greater longevity, higher functional ability, or lower rates of depression. These findings are particularly relevant today as baby boomers—the generation of 77 million Americans born between 1946 and 1964—reach the age typically associated with retirement. We know that baby boomers in their late 40s to mid-50s are volunteering at a higher rate than earlier generations did at the same age. However, efforts should be made to not only maintain current levels of volunteering among baby boomers, but to keep those baby boomers who already volunteer serving in the future by providing substantial, challenging, and fulfilling volunteer experiences. The results of such efforts will not only help solve community problems, but simultaneously enhance the health of the growing number of older adults.

Periodical Bibliography

The following articles have been selected to supplement the diverse views presented in this chapter.

Jack Gillum — "College Grads Going to 'Work' for New Orleans," *USA Today*, June 19, 2006.

Glamour — "Volunteer This Summer! It'll Pay You Back in Surprising Ways," June 2010.

B. Allison Gray — "The Call to Service," *Library Journal*, July 15, 2009.

Julia Howell — "Giving Gives Back: The Benefits of Giving and Volunteering," *Maclean's*, October 6, 2008

Marjorie Ingall — "What Goes Around Comes Around," *Self*, December 2008.

Nicholas D. Kristof — "Our Basic Human Pleasures: Food, Sex and Giving," *New York Times*, January 17, 2010.

Cassie Moore — "Alumni of National-Service Program Continue to Get Involved in Volunteering," *Chronicle of Philanthropy*, May 13, 2008.

Theresa Tighe — "As Volunteers Age, Charities Are Finding Fewer and Fewer Young Replacements," *St. Louis Post-Dispatch*, December 2, 2005.

Alina Tugend — "The Benefits of Volunteerism, if the Service Is Real," *New York Times*, July 31, 2010.

CHAPTER 3

What Role Should Service Learning Play in Society?

Chapter Preface

While definitions of service learning vary, according to Learn and Serve America, one of the federal programs administered by the Corporation for National and Community Service, service learning is "a teaching and learning strategy that integrates meaningful community service with instruction and reflection to enrich the learning experience, teach civic responsibility, and strengthen communities."[1] Because many believe that service learning makes better citizens and improves communities, some suggest that service learning should be required for high school graduation. While several states encourage service learning and some include service learning in their education standards, only one state, Maryland, mandates that students must perform community service in conjunction with an academic course to graduate from high school. Opposition to such policies is strong, and the controversy is one of the hottest issues in the service-learning debate.

Those who oppose mandatory service learning in high school do so for many of the same reasons that people oppose mandatory national service in general. Opponents argue that service should always be a personal choice and that any form of mandatory service is un-American and diminishes the meaning of true volunteerism. The parents of fourteen-year-old Aric Herndon of Chapel Hill, North Carolina, went to court to oppose the school district's community service requirement. They argued that the community service policy violated their right to direct the upbringing and education of their son. They also claimed that the policy violated their son's constitutional right to be free from involuntary servitude. The Fourth US Circuit Court of Appeals upheld the

---

1. The National Service-Learning Clearinghouse, "Frequently Asked Questions," accessed on December 4, 2010. www.servicelearning.org.

lower court ruling that rejected the parents' claims. In its decision, the circuit court held that while the US Supreme Court has ruled that parents have a liberty interest in their children's schooling that is protected by the Fourteenth Amendment, the Supreme Court has also declared that even if in conflict with parental interest, schooling is subject to reasonable regulation by the state. Asking students to perform a moderate amount of community service is reasonable, the circuit court concluded. The court also rejected the claim that mandatory community service was involuntary servitude. "There is no basis in fact or logic which would support analogizing a mandatory community service program in a public high school to slavery."[2]

Even some who generally oppose any form of compulsory national service for adults often support mandatory service for high school graduation. According to Michael Lind, a fellow at the New America Foundation, "There's nothing wrong with requiring students to do something for their community."[3] Lind asserts that learning the value of helping others is an appropriate goal of education. "Education is not simply memorizing and regurgitating data but training students to be good citizens, helping them acquire the habit of good citizenship early."[4] Moreover, supporters argue, students enrolled in public school are wards of the state. Therefore, the state can make a public school student's graduation contingent upon a mandatory service requirement if it sees fit to do so. "Bringing groceries to poor people, restoring the environment, tutoring younger kids—such activities are all part of the legitimate educational mission of school."[5]

The mandatory service-learning issue remains hotly contested. The authors in the chapter that follows add their views

2. *Herndon v. Chapel Hill-Carrboro City Board of Education*, 89 F.3d 174 (4th Cir. 1996).
3. Quoted in "National Service," John Greenya, *CQ Researcher*, June 30, 2006.
4. *Ibid.*
5. *Ibid.*

to this debate and explore other issues related to service learning. As more states and school districts consider mandatory service requirements, those who have studied Maryland's mandatory service program suggest that more research is needed to evaluate its impact. In her 2006 doctoral thesis, Sara Helms, now a professor of economics at the University of Alabama, cautions, "We need more information on whether these programs are doing what [education policy makers] think they are doing."[6]

---

6. Sara Helms, "Involuntary Volunteering: The Impact of Mandated Service in Public Schools," University of Maryland, June 2006.

| "Through careful course management
and the embedding of service-learning,
we have the opportunity to change
people's attitudes from 'What's in it for
me?' to 'How can I help?'"

Service Learning Makes Students into Better Citizens

Michael G. Hypes

*Michael G. Hypes argues in the following viewpoint that service
learning not only enriches a student's learning experience but
also teaches civic responsibility. Rather than seeking to enhance
their careers, many young professionals seek only the immediate
benefits of service, he claims. One way to change this attitude is
to incorporate service learning into course work, Hypes asserts.
To open students' eyes to the needs of their communities, educators nationwide have the responsibility to motivate their students
through service learning, he maintains. Hypes, professor of sports
management at Morehead State University, in Kentucky, is chair
of the* Journal of Physical Education, Recreation & Dance *editorial board.*

Michael G. Hypes, "What's in It for Me?" *JOPERD—Journal of Physical Education,
Recreation & Dance*, vol. 80, November–December 2009. Reproduced by permission.

As you read, consider the following questions:

1. Why, in Hypes's opinion, is service learning such a hot topic?

2. According to the author, what do today's young professionals and students not understand?

3. What, in the author's view, is the core concept that drives the service learning educational strategy?

Over the past 25 years or more in higher education, I have seen many trends come and go. The world of education is filled with buzzwords and ideas that define a given time period in educational theory and thought. As the profession progresses into the new millennium, one of the trends is the renewed emphasis on service-learning, civic engagement, and servant leadership.

Service-learning can be defined as a teaching and learning strategy that integrates meaningful community service with instruction and reflection to enrich the learning experience, teach civic responsibility, and strengthen communities. Integration of service-learning activities or components can be found across the nation at all levels, elementary through higher education. Civic engagement comprises individual and collective actions designed to identify and address issues of public concern.

The "What's in It for Me" Attitude

Why is service-learning such a hot topic? Personal observation and research results indicate a decline in volunteerism across the country. Activities or causes that people used to be involved in have declined because of the "what's in it for me" attitude. I have observed this among my students, as well as among many professionals in the field. During my academic preparation, active participation in professional organizations was not just recommended, it was expected. The opportunity to be involved in the direction of the field, to be active in leadership positions, and to have the opportunity for scholarly pursuits provided for involvement and a chance to give back to the profession.

Today's young professionals and students do not understand the opportunities they have in professional organizations and the profession. They are interested only in the immediate benefits, such as being paid to deliver a workshop at a state, regional, or national conference or having their travel paid to attend the meeting. Gone is the broader vision of bringing about change. This mind-set has contributed to stagnation in the profession. When encouraged to become a member, one of the students' first questions is "What's in it for me?" How do we get back to true professional development and encourage young professionals to enhance the profession and to actively seek leadership responsibilities?

One avenue is through the incorporation of service-learning activities in their course work. Through service-learning, students provide an important service to the community while at the same time learning about educational analysis, developing an understanding of education issues, learning to interpret these issues, and practicing communication skills by speaking to residents. They may also reflect on their personal and career interests in education, the environment, public policy, or other related areas. In these ways service-learning intentionally combines service with learning, a combination that can transform both students and communities.

A Transformative Teaching Method

So, "What's in it for me?" The core concept that drives this educational strategy is that the combination of service and learning objectives, with the intent to show measurable change in both the recipient and the provider of the service, results in a radically transformative method of teaching students. Com-

Countries with National Youth Service Policies

- Bolivia

- Brazil

- China

- Colombia

- Costa Rica

- Djibouti

- Dominican Republic

- Ghana

- Honduras

- Italy

- Malaysia

- Mexico

- New Guinea

- Nicaragua

- Nigeria

- Panama

- Philippines

- Venezuela

Innovations in Civic Participation, www.icicp.org.

munity members, students, and educators everywhere are discovering that service-learning offers all its participants a chance to take part in the active education of youths while simultaneously addressing the concerns, needs, and hopes of their community and the profession as a whole.

It is the responsibility of educators to motivate students. Service-learning provides a means of opening the eyes of students to major issues in the field and giving them the opportunity to make a difference. Through careful course management and the embedding of service-learning, we have the opportunity to change people's attitudes from "What's in it for me?" to "How can I help?"

"By attempting to substitute emotions for reason, service-learning contravenes the purpose of liberal education while chipping away at students' respect for the social order."

Service Learning Does Not Make Students into Better Citizens

John B. Egger

In the following viewpoint, John B. Egger claims that if teaching students to be better citizens is the goal, service learning is not the solution. In fact, he argues, service learning weakens respect for society by teaching students that they are responsible for those whose hardships they had no role in creating. A traditional liberal education that helps students understand human nature and the value of mutual respect and social cooperation is a better way to teach civic responsibility, Egger maintains. Service learning does not encourage learning but exploits students to promote a communitarian, anti-individualist social agenda, he concludes. Egger is a professor of economics at Towson University in Maryland.

John B. Egger, "No Service to Learning: 'Service-Learning' Reappraised," *Academic Questions*, vol. 21, 2008, pp. 183–194. Reproduced with kind permission from Springer Science and Business Media and the author.

As you read, consider the following questions:

1. According to Egger, why do the best-known goals of service learning make it difficult for a well-meaning scholar to dispute them?

2. What does the author assert is chipping away at liberal education?

3. In the author's view, why is promoting reliance on one's emotions contrary to the university's mission?

Mixing community service with college students' learning is a bad idea. When service-learning was promoted in a newspaper op-ed by Dr. Robert L. Caret, the president of Towson University (where I have taught for over two decades), I responded skeptically. Dr. Caret's follow-up letter suggested that I misunderstood service-learning.

I argued that wrapping a veneer of learning over community service conceals the promotion of a particular social agenda, that it wastes students' valuable time and other resources, and that its learning goal actually weakens students' respect for the processes of social interaction that is conveyed by a good liberal education.

Like many op-eds, mine was written quickly, but I think a closer look reveals no substantive problem: Service-learning attempts to promote a communitarian, anti-individualistic social agenda, and the attempt and agenda are educationally harmful. . . .

The Goals of Service-Learning

A perfidious aspect of service-learning is that its best-known goals seem so benevolent that no well-meaning scholar could dispute them: Civility and "empathy for others" are hard to quarrel with, and "civic responsibility" and "commitment to the community" might simply refer to an acceptance of one's role in maintaining institutions that facilitate social cooperation. "The greater good" and "overcoming self-absorption" are more problematic, and suggest the true ideological goal of service-learning. Well-intentioned professors drawn to the technique for its contributions to civility and empathy may find themselves inadvertently contributing to these more extreme goals.

If civility were the primary goal of service-learning advocates—it was first on Caret's list—they need look no further than the traditional liberal education. Promoting a work ethic, second on his list, is part and parcel of such an education, but it is work befitting a student: reading, thinking, and writing, not the unskilled labor of digging tires from streams or dishing out soup.

Promoting Civility

A liberal education offers courses like history, chemistry, calculus, and music appreciation that promote the student's understanding of human nature and therefore his ability to cooperate with others in a society. In the early days of the West's transition to liberalism, economists like Adam Smith—in his 1759 *The Theory of Moral Sentiments* as well as *The Wealth of Nations*—and other political scientists reasoned that there is no conflict between properly understood self-interest, within a moral and legal framework respecting individuals' autonomy and rights, and a love of society. Indeed, economists maintain that an individual's respect for society arises from self-interest, from the benefits *to one's self* that social cooperation makes possible. In a free society, each makes himself better off by making others better off, with the strengthening of social bonds and mutual respect among people an unintended but inevitable consequence.

An education that promotes civility has, therefore, nothing to do with "good works," the service part of service-learning. If students are thought to "lack civility or a traditional work ethic," and to be "too self-absorbed" in not appreciating the importance of considering others, a liberal education that teaches the advantages of respecting others' nature as human beings, of trading with them, and of contributing to the civic institutions on which any free society depends would remedy that.

A Recommitment to True Liberal Education

The modern student, tragically, too often is not being taught these lessons, as liberal education is chipped away by various "studies" that promote the special interests of particular groups and denigrate the individualism of Western political philosophy. Among the consequences are disrespectful behavior that arises from students' ignorance of the social function of morals, manners, and culture, and their widespread misunderstanding and distrust of human freedom—especially free markets. Teachers who instill these lessons do their students no favors. Their advocacy of service-learning may reflect an awareness that the very changes they have wrought in undergraduate education have rendered civility and respect for others less common. If these are truly their goals, the remedy is not service-learning, a makeshift substitute that diverts attention and resources from liberal education and reinforces *antiliberal* attitudes. It is a recommitment to true liberal education.

Civility, liberal education teaches, requires the respectful treatment of strangers because of their nature as fellow human beings, but it does not require giving each of them one's money or labor. Far from losing "sight of the greater good," it teaches that one's civil self-interested action best furthers it. Students should, of course, not be discouraged from using leisure for activities like stream cleaning, but they should not be substitutes for academic work. The "greater good" is better furthered by development of skills in which students have a comparative advantage, in the library, lab, or classroom. They further their own interests by increasing the value of the services they are able to provide to others.

Although most economists—whose subject, after all, is based on what Smith called "self-love"—embrace the principle that enlightened self-interest promotes civility, and Caret's letter referred to it as a "truism," this interpretation is not universal. Certainly the kind of self-interest that is unconstrained by the proper moral and legal structure can be antisocial. Those who disagree that civility is subsumed by self-interest must treat that powerful motive as something to be reined in by morality, law, and respect for others. Civilized people, in this view, learn the virtue of acting morally and civilly, even though this is contrary to their self-interest. Certainly a liberal education can promote civility and respect in this way, but its clash with the economist's (well, *this* economist's) perspective is sharp. In either case, genuine learning of this lesson is not the goal of service-learning.

Weakening Respect for Society

Service-learning's goal may not in fact be civility and "commitment to the community" in the sense of liberal education's understanding of human society's contribution to the individual's flourishing. It may, instead, be the promotion of a communitarian ethic that suppresses and denigrates the individual in favor of a group or "society" and views self-interest as a vice. From this perspective, social order can coexist with individualism—it's hard to deny that the West has prospered since the Enlightenment—but it is a mean social order not consistent with human beings at their best.

This position's ethic, a guiding principle of service-learning, actually weakens respect for society. Teaching that others are morally entitled to a part of one's life—people one does not know, may not like, and whose misfortune one had no role in creating—is a sure way to engender a sense of resentment and disdain, not benevolence, toward one's fellow human beings. In the ethic consistent with the West's liberal traditions, one views others benevolently because association with them can make one better off. This source of benevolence is replaced by suspicion and distrust when others' misfortunes constitute a moral claim on one's own life. This is how the central lesson of service-learning weakens the very social fabric its supporters believe they are promoting.

Liberal education has a place for the study of socialist or communitarian ethics: in courses of philosophy, history, political science, and economics where logical reasoning deduces conclusions from underlying axioms. This is profoundly not the method of service-learning, which conceals behind a façade of learning an appeal to students' emotions.

Training the Mind

A university's purpose is to train the mind. Promoting reliance on one's emotions, even if they are supported by reason but particularly if they supplant or even contradict it, is profoundly contrary to the university's mission. A professor can convey, in a few minutes at most, the discipline-related intellectual content of most service-learning assignments, but the "learning" at which service-learning aims with, say, a student's hours in a soup kitchen, is not intellectual: It's simply the emotional experience. These feelings provide no clue to the actual amelioration of poverty. Would a higher minimum wage help? How about tax laws that permit the expensing of capital investments? With credit hours the real student is not accumulating in the soup kitchen, she can analyze these policy changes. That's what education is for.

But the reasoned analysis of the causes and effects of "community needs" is not the goal of service-learning. Nor is "serendipitous learning" about one's career. Service-learning seeks to exploit young students' natural sympathy for the less fortunate, relying on emotions to promote a socialist, communitarian philosophy. By attempting to substitute emotions for reason, service-learning contravenes the purpose of liberal education while chipping away at students' respect for the social order. Despite its name, service-learning does no service to learning.

> "Volunteers, as any nonprofit leader will
> tell you (off the record, for fear of look-
> ing a gift horse . . .) can be as much a
> curse as a blessing."

Service Learning Can
Be a Burden for Some
Service Organizations

Stephanie Strom

*In the following viewpoint, Stephanie Strom claims that for
many organizations, service-learning volunteers are more a burden than a help, particularly when the academic institution has
not adequately coordinated the project. In many cases, she asserts, the person who must supervise service-learning volunteers
already has significant responsibilities. Moreover, Strom maintains, some claim that the students have too little time to devote
to justify the resources organizations must devote to adequately
train them. Increasingly, however, academic institutions have developed offices to better oversee service-learning projects and thus
better help the organizations that students serve. Strom covers
nonprofit groups and philanthropy for the* New York Times.

As you read, consider the following questions:

1. According to Strom, how did an information technology capstone course at the University of Massachusetts improve the service-learning experience at Enlace de Familias?

2. When does the author assert service learning took off?

3. What did the director of academic service learning at the University of Texas, Austin, do to solidify expectations on both sides of the service-learning project?

Betty Medina Lichtenstein used to dread the beginning of the school year, when students from colleges and universities around Holyoke, Mass., would descend on her tiny community organization, Enlace de Familias.

"Suddenly, droves of students were walking through my door, interrupting my day and asking, 'What can I do here?'" she says. "A whole other crowd would send résumé after résumé after résumé expecting me to call them back. Still other ones would come in and say, 'How about some research on X?' in August and then show up in late October saying their thesis really needed to be about Y.

"It was total havoc."

This year [2010], Ms. Medina Lichtenstein feels better about service learning. For their information technology capstone course at the University of Massachusetts, Amherst, two students created a Web site and database management system that allow Ms. Medina Lichtenstein to complete in one day an annual report that used to take a week. Another two students embarked on an assessment of Enlace's information technology system with the aim of making it better.

Working with the students required just a few hours of Ms. Medina Lichtenstein's time. For the students, says Carol Soules, their professor, "it was a great practical experience, but a whole other aspect of it is that it helped them to see what the digital divide means in real life."

Ms. Medina Lichtenstein's experiences illustrate the good and the bad of service learning, loosely defined as community service that supplements and enhances what students learn in a classroom.

As Much a Curse as a Blessing

Volunteers, as any nonprofit leader will tell you (off the record, for fear of looking a gift horse . . .), can be as much a curse as a blessing, especially to an organization that lacks the administrative structure and money to train and supervise students. Some organizations pay a coordinator to direct volunteers, but most consider that a luxury they cannot afford.

"It's not unusual for the task of supervising students to fall to someone who already has plenty of responsibilities," says Elizabeth A. Tryon, the community learning coordinator at the Morgridge Center for Public Service at the University of Wisconsin, Madison. "If service learning is not well coordinated by the academic institution, it can place a lot of burden on the community partner."

A positive experience usually requires a considerable investment of time and planning on the part of academic institutions and faculty. Ideally, service learning enriches a particular course of study, and students have the opportunity to reflect in the classroom on their experiences. In reality, service learning often seems unconnected to any curriculum—painting park benches, for example. At its most basic, it can be hard to distinguish from plain vanilla community service.

"The best service learning really involves a process something like old-fashioned matchmaking," says Andrea Dolan-Potter, whose former job as assistant director of the East Madison Community Center in Wisconsin exposed her to service learning.

Questioning the Benefits
of Service Learning

This town/gown divide is explored in *The Unheard Voices: Community Organizations and Service Learning*, published last summer by Temple University Press and mostly written by students at the University of Wisconsin who, as part of a research seminar, interviewed staff members of 64 nonprofit organizations.

Some community leaders spoke of student volunteers having too little time to get much meaningful experience or to justify a significant investment of time to train them. Others told of students arriving on their doorsteps with little guidance or preparation from their professors and expecting to change the world in 20 hours over a single semester. Some felt that their clients were guinea pigs for students doing research, without any return for them.

"Academic institutions are focused on making sure their students learn from the service-learning experience, but they aren't always paying similar attention to the interests of the organizations that provide that experience, much less the clients they serve," says Randy Stoecker, a professor at the University of Wisconsin, who edited the book with Ms. Tryon.

Arriving as the [Barack] Obama administration is making volunteerism and other forms of civic engagement a cornerstone of its higher-education agenda, the book raises questions about how much benefit results from student efforts. That's something that Karen Sánchez-Eppler, a professor at Amherst College, has wondered about. Two decades ago, Ms. Sánchez-Eppler made community service part of her syllabus for "Reading, Writing and Teaching," a required English course. Every semester, some of her students spend 20 hours assisting teachers at Holyoke High School in Holyoke, Mass. They help struggling students, supervise a student group putting out a poetry magazine and conduct writing workshops. Last year, 25 teachers applied for eight tutors from the class.

"That program has been useful to individual kids there and supporting and invigorating for the teachers," Ms. Sánchez-Eppler says, "but it really has had little to no institutional impact. During the 20 years of this course, the school has continued to have high dropout rates, low test scores, high teen pregnancy rates."

Holyoke High has far less lofty expectations. "A program of her size would have minimal impact," David Dupont, the principal, says. "However, just the fact that her students are benefiting along with ours to any degree is worth having it at Holyoke High School."

The Cart Before the Horse

"The horse got a little before the cart," says Ms. Soules, who in addition to teaching directs service learning at the University of Massachusetts, Amherst. "The concept of service learning really took off before the infrastructure was in place to support it," she says.

Last academic year, more than 3,000 students at her campus engaged in service learning under the tutelage of 67 professors teaching 105 courses. Ms. Soules would prefer that all of those experiences occur in small courses spanning a year, so that students have time to immerse themselves, but she knows that is not possible. "We have all different levels of service learning," she says. "When it takes place in an introductory course with a hundred students who are spending two hours a week, sometimes they do end up answering phones, filing, sweeping the floors and sorting clothes."

"But," she adds, "it gives them exposure to different communities, which is valuable, and in fact those are the things many nonprofits need done."

It was in the mid-1980s that service learning took off, with the establishment of organizations like Campus Compact and Youth Service America, whose mission is to spur national service efforts among youth. Today, most colleges and universi-

The Usefulness of Service Learning

Effective	Ineffective
• Mandates fair distribution of service placements to all neighborhoods that are part of the community. • Organizes a system for instructing students about service and for coordinating effective placement in cooperation with community partner. • Provides helpful and typically low-cost labor by undergraduate students • Provides graduate-student expertise to address community-partner staff • Views students as role models for the constituencies being served by community partner • Hires students to become employees of the community partner	• Discriminates against providing student service in areas based on race, class, and safety concerns • Permits sense of student entitlement • Fails to recognize that under-prepared undergraduate students tax community partner personnel, placing an increased strain on the infrastructure • Shifts service-learning purpose from community-centered to student-centered • Treats community partners as merely a laboratory • Depends on community partner excessively, resulting in too many students calling for interviews, information, and placement

TAKEN FROM: Sean Creighton, "Significant Findings in Campus-Community Engagement: Community Partner Perspective," *Journal for Civic Commitment*, 2008.

ties incorporate service learning in their curriculums, and some departments require at least one course; in 2008, Tulane made a service-learning course part of the required core curriculum.

No one knows how many students participate in service learning nationwide, but 1.2 million students and 22,000 community organizations are involved in programs with grants from the Corporation for National and Community Service, a government agency that is perhaps the largest financer of programs.

Elson B. Nash, the acting director of the agency's Learn and Serve America program, says its grants are aimed at encouraging a better experience for academic institutions and their nonprofit partners. "The relationships are key because everyone—the students, faculty and community organization—needs to be involved in developing the expectations for the service-learning experience," Mr. Nash says. "They need to talk about what it's going to address, how the students are going to be involved, how it connects to the classroom experience, how it meets the nonprofit's needs and, most importantly, how it is going to be evaluated."

Establishing Partnerships

More and more universities are establishing offices to oversee programs and otherwise formalize what has until recently been an ad hoc experiment in civic engagement. "It's a very fragile relationship between the academic institution and the community organization," says Lanese Aggrey, director of academic service learning at the University of Texas, Austin. "We need to stop looking at it as a one-dimensional thing and start building a real partnership."

When she arrived to take up her post at the University of Texas a year and a half ago, only three courses were listed as having service learning. "What I found was, we really are the land of orange tape," she says, referring to the school colors. Professors wanting to add service learning had to get approval from four different officials. Instead, the professors incorporated service learning informally, which made it harder for the university to track and assess programs.

After eliminating three of the four hurdles, the university quickly accumulated 45 courses that included service learning; in three of them students travel abroad. The goal is 100 such classes.

The university asks participating students and nonprofit groups to sign a contract that spells out dates and hours of service, what service will be provided, and a commitment by the nonprofit to evaluate the student at the conclusion of service. "It's a good way to solidify expectations on both sides," Dr. Aggrey says. "It helps the community partner understand that its needs may only be met to a certain extent, because students have limited time and other obligations, and it helps students understand they can't just blow off their service-learning commitments to go have pizza and beer."

A Career-Changing Experience

Consider what went into planning and executing Anne Witt's service-learning experience in the summer of 2007. Now a junior at the University of Notre Dame, Ms. Witt worked as a counselor at a camp run by Gwen's Girls, which provides a range of services to at-risk girls in the Pittsburgh area.

The process of placing her began six months earlier when, under Notre Dame's Urban Plunge program, students made the rounds of social service agencies in Pittsburgh to see if they might find summer service. One student interested in medicine went to work for a health clinic; another considering a legal career got a position at an immigration office.

Ms. Witt chose Gwen's Girls. "I'm a political science major, so law school was what was on my radar," she says. "But after working with Gwen's Girls, I realize there are so many problems with education in Pittsburgh, and that's made me more interested in teaching." One girl, for instance, thought Jamaica was a state and Africa was just south of the United States. "These girls lived 20 minutes away from my home," Ms. Witt says, "but the disparity between what I got out of my education and what they had was huge."

Each week, Ms. Witt had relevant reading to do and papers to write. When she got back to school in the fall, she and other students in the program got together to discuss their experiences and the social issues involved.

The Notre Dame Club of Pittsburgh, an alumni group, hosted a breakfast for students doing service learning and the organizations they were working with. The club also awarded Ms. Witt a $2,000 scholarship to compensate for a summer without income. A staff member from Notre Dame's Center for Social Concerns, which oversees the Urban Plunge program, dropped in, too, to see what the students were doing. "These people are so interested in supporting these kids and making sure they really get something out of this experience," says Lynn Knezevich, executive director of Gwen's Girls.

The organization also benefited. It got a volunteer camp counselor who ended up going back as a paid counselor this summer.

But just as important to Ms. Knezevich was the opportunity to expose her students to a broader world. "You're not necessarily learning this for your class credits," she says. "You may be doing this to learn about different and diverse populations, which may not have anything to do with what your major is but will educate you as a person."

| "Service learning should 'really help' both the student and the organization she serves."

Service Learning Must Meet the Needs of Students and the Served Organizations

Stan Katz

For service-learning programs to be effective, they must serve both students and served organizations, argues Stan Katz in the following viewpoint. Unfortunately, achieving both goals can be a challenge, he asserts. The instructor must design a course where service is well integrated with course content, and the organization must provide a meaningful task for the student volunteers to complete, Katz claims. Suggestions that the service-learning process be more formalized may defeat this purpose, as creativity is needed to meet service learning's dual objectives, he maintains. Katz, a regular blogger for the Chronicle of Higher Education, *directs the Center for Arts and Cultural Policy Studies at Princeton University.*

Stan Katz, "Does Service Learning Really Help?" *Chronicle of Higher Education*, January 12, 2010. Reproduced by permission of the author.

As you read, consider the following questions:

1. What does Katz claim is the general wisdom among nonprofit service organizations concerning student volunteers?

2. What does the author assert is a false dichotomy?

3. What has the author learned based on his limited experience with service learning?

S everal days ago, Stephanie Strom of the *New York Times* asked, "Does service learning really help?" It's a good question. Ms. Strom, whose beat for the *Times* is philanthropy, focused mainly on the question of whether the students engaged in service learning are really benefitting the nonprofit service organizations they are trying to assist. Not surprisingly, some of her respondents who run the nonprofits were not so sure that their student volunteers were worth the effort that necessarily goes into supervising them. This is the general wisdom concerning volunteers, and there is no reason to think that student service learners would be different from other volunteers.

Strom's article was stimulated by a recent publication emanating from the University of Wisconsin, which runs the Morgridge Center for Public Service. Elizabeth Tryon, its service learning coordinator, is quoted as saying that "if service learning is not well coordinated by the academic institution, it can be a burden on the community partner," and that seems obvious. Strom comments that "a positive experience usually requires a considerable investment of time and planning on the part of academic institutions and faculty. Ideally, service learning enriches a particular course of study, and students have the opportunity to reflect in the classroom on their experiences." I would certainly hope so, but Strom goes on to say

Service-Learning Star Parties

Telescopes were set up in the football field [on the Nevada-Oregon border] and pointed toward the vast nighttime sky. High school students designed exhibits about the solar system in the gym for visitors to pass through before gathering outside on the field. The older students also teamed up with elementary students to help the younger kids explain to visitors what they'd learned about the universe and to share Native American lore. . . .

At the "star parties," students also perform Native American dances wearing traditional attire. . . .

Mary Baird [science teacher and service-learning coordinator] says the star parties have not only brought the tribe closer to its culture, they've increased pride and empowered the community to build on the momentum created by the students [bringing in tourists to boost the local economy was a goal]. . . .

"The real strength of service-learning is in allowing the kids to develop and plan out their own ideas, and to build stronger ties to the community through their schoolwork," says Baird. "The payoff is the growth you see in the kids. It's incredible."

Cindy Long,
"Making the Connection,"
NEA Today, *November 2007.*

that "in reality, service learning often seems unconnected to any curriculum—painting park benches, for example. At its most basic, it can be hard to distinguish from plain vanilla community service."

A Tight Integration of Service and Course Content

I suppose there may be a context in which a committed instructor could turn "painting park benches" into a teachable moment, but I have long thought that the community-service component of service learning ought to be tightly integrated into the subject-matter content of the service-learning course. Sometimes, of course, the "content" will be a process. Strom cites as an example an innovative English professor, Karen Sánchez-Eppler, whose Amherst College students in a required course on "Reading, Writing and Teaching" assist high school English teachers in nearby Holyoke, Mass., helping to put out a poetry magazine and running writing workshops. A more traditional content-related example of service learning would be the history professor whose students volunteer at a local soup kitchen and conduct oral histories of its clients for a social history of their community.

But the question posed by my example would be: How great a help to the managers of the soup kitchen would the history students be? Which comes first, the service or the learning? The obvious response is that this is a false dichotomy [division], for in a successful service-learning environment, both objectives are attained simultaneously—useful service is performed for the nonprofit organization, while structured analysis of the service experience forms a significant part of student learning.

My own limited experience with service learning suggests that it is difficult to achieve both goals. The academic course must be well designed and managed by the instructor, the nonprofit must provide a meaningful task environment for the volunteer, and there must be a strong fit between the classroom and the nonprofit environment. Strom concludes that universities must strive to "formalize what has until recently been an ad hoc experiment in civic engagement." I am sure that is generally correct, but my fear is that in formalizing, we may be killing the goose that laid the golden egg. I think it must be quite difficult to maintain the creativity and spontaneity that a continuing series of positive cognitive experiences will require. We mustn't forget the "learning" in service learning—and I suspect that we need to continue to explore new methods of assessing the outcomes of service-learning experiences. In principle, service learning should "really help" both the student and the organization she serves.

> "Service learning . . . is a powerful tool
> to keep students on track to graduate
> from high school."

Service Learning Improves Graduation Rates

John Bridgeland

In a nationwide survey, 64 percent of service-learning students said that service learning would have a significant impact on their decision to stay in school, claims John Bridgeland in the following viewpoint. Unfortunately, service-learning programs are still rare. Dropouts want to see the real-world relevance of what they learn in the classroom, Bridgeland maintains. Service learning can make the connection between the classroom and a career and should therefore receive more support to help reduce the nation's dropout rate. Bridgeland, the chief executive officer of Civic Enterprises, is coauthor of the book The Silent Epidemic: Perspectives of High School Dropouts.

As you read, consider the following questions:

1. According to Bridgeland, how many students drop out of school each day?

John Bridgeland, "The Key to Keeping Teens in School," *Christian Science Monitor*, April 15, 2008, p. 9. Reproduced by permission of the author.

2. What does the author claim jolted the nation to act on educational and civic challenges?

3. In the author's view, what federal program should target the dropout problem?

Every day, 7 thousand high school students drop out of school—and the American high school graduation rate hasn't budged for almost three decades. In an effort to jumpstart those rates, General Colin Powell recently announced the development of 100 dropout prevention summits across the US.

On the heels of that step comes even more hope for reducing the number of dropouts and it includes the needed spawning of more civic engagement among young people.

Service learning is an educational technique that combines classroom learning with community service. What's critical is that it is not only key to getting more students engaged in their communities, but, according to a report released last week by Civic Enterprises, it is also a powerful tool to keep students on track to graduate from high school.

A Hopeful Picture

A nationally representative survey of high school students, including at-risk students, paints a hopeful picture. Eighty-two percent of all service-learning students said their view of school improved because of their service-learning classes, and 77 percent said that service learning had a big effect on motivating them to work hard. Furthermore, 64 percent of service-learning students claimed that service learning would have a fairly or very big effect on keeping them from dropping out of school.

Dropout crisis reforms combat a number of barriers—they must increase attendance, student motivation, engagement, [and] academic performance, and create learning environments free of disruptive behavior. Research shows that service learning accomplishes each of these.

Although high-quality service-learning programs are cropping up across the nation, such programs are still unjustifiably rare. Eighty-three percent of students said that if their school offered it, they would enroll in a service-learning program. Yet only 16 percent of all students, and only 8 percent of students at low-performing schools, reported that their schools offered service learning. All too often students do not have access to, or do not even know about, such programs offered by their schools.

This latest survey builds on two groundbreaking 2006 reports that jolted the nation to act on educational and civic challenges. One report showed that nearly one-third of all high school students fail to graduate with their class and almost half of all minority students drop out before graduation. Meanwhile, America's Civic Health Index [by the National Conference on Citizenship] showed that high school dropouts hardly participated in civic duties—declining to vote, volunteer, or advocate for reforming schools that were failing them. Addressing these twin challenges of high school dropout and civic disengagement requires comprehensive reform aimed at making school more rigorous, relevant, and engaging.

Targeting the Dropout Problem

Enter service learning. As school districts, states, and the federal government debate how to best address the US dropout crisis, service learning should be at the forefront of strategies used to raise graduation rates.

Learn and Serve America, the federal program that annually provides from $34 to $43 million in grants to K–12 schools, should target the dropout problem. All AmeriCorps volunteers who serve in disadvantaged public schools with high dropout rates should be trained as service-learning coordinators and help teachers implement high-quality programs.

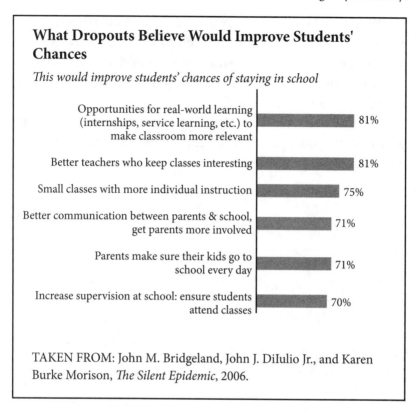

What Dropouts Believe Would Improve Students' Chances

This would improve students' chances of staying in school

Opportunities for real-world learning (internships, service learning, etc.) to make classroom more relevant	81%
Better teachers who keep classes interesting	81%
Small classes with more individual instruction	75%
Better communication between parents & school, get parents more involved	71%
Parents make sure their kids go to school every day	71%
Increase supervision at school: ensure students attend classes	70%

TAKEN FROM: John M. Bridgeland, John J. DiIulio Jr., and Karen Burke Morison, *The Silent Epidemic*, 2006.

The White House coordinating council for national and community service should charge programs across government with making service learning in schools a priority for their programs.

It wouldn't be a stretch for programs such as the [US] National Park Service to take up that task. After all, it has 200,000 volunteers and federally supported mentoring programs at the Departments of Education and Health and Human Services.

Dropouts want to see the connection between classroom learning and a career. Communities suffer from an absence of their civic talents. Service learning can bridge the divide between these two issues. It is an essential tool to address our nation's dropout challenge, keep students engaged in school, and prepare them for the duties of citizenship.

As Sen. Edward Kennedy put it, "We need students who graduate from high school prepared to succeed in today's global economy. We also need students who understand the value of service and of helping others—whether in their own communities or across the world."

Imagine a movement in America that focuses on turning potential dropouts into model citizens. Service learning is that movement.

> "[Research service-learning] students explore topics more deeply and directly experience the complexity, hard work, frustrations, and rewards of doing science."

Service Learning Increases Science Literacy

Julie A. Reynolds and Jennifer Ahern-Dodson

In the following viewpoint, Julie A. Reynolds and Jennifer Ahern-Dodson assert that research service learning is an excellent way to promote science literacy. Research service learning helps students understand the demands of scientific research, cultivate critical-thinking skills, and increase understanding of environmental issues, the authors claim. Not only do students benefit by studying authentic scientific questions, but communities also get answers to pressing environmental questions, they reason. Reynolds is director of the Certificate in Teaching College Biology at Duke University in Durham, North Carolina. Ahern-Dodson is civic engagement consultant and writing instructor at Duke.

As you read, consider the following questions:

1. What are some examples of traditional service-learning activities?

2. In the authors' opinion, what do the critiques of service learning include?

3. According to the authors, how can colleges and universities benefit from research service learning?

Science literacy is often narrowly construed as the understanding of key concepts and principles of science when, as Carl Sagan said, "Science is a way of thinking much more than it is a body of knowledge." [F.J.] Rutherford and [A.] Ahlgren (1991) argued that scientifically literate people should understand the strengths and limitations of science, be familiar with the diversity and unity of nature, and be able to use scientific thinking and knowledge. Given this idea, we wondered how much undergraduate science courses actually promote science literacy. Certainly many do, particularly upper-division courses. But many introductory courses probably do not promote science literacy, especially when they focus on covering content. Paradoxically, introductory courses have both the greatest opportunity to promote science literacy—because so many students take them—and the greatest potential to perpetuate the myth that science is inaccessible to the average person—by focusing on content.

Therefore, when we decided to design an introductory course for non-majors that would promote science literacy, we knew we should move beyond content and teach students to think scientifically. Our solution was to use an emerging pedagogy, research service-learning (RSL), to engage students in authentic, community-based scientific research while showing them how to use their new knowledge to serve society.

Research as Service

Traditional service-learning is a form of experiential education in which students engage in activities that address human and community needs and then reflect on those service experiences through structured opportunities designed to promote learning and development. Examples of service-learning activities include tutoring academically at-risk students, working in food banks, and visiting older adults in nursing homes.

RSL expands this model to include research as service. RSL teaches students to ask research questions that are relevant to their communities' needs and to work with faculty and community partners to design and implement research projects to address those needs. This approach encourages students to investigate why service is needed and to consider the larger institutional structures that impact their project. Service is linked to the themes of the course (e.g., emerging diseases or impacts of technology on society) and students learn basic research skills such as conducting literature reviews, identifying research questions, taking field notes, gathering and analyzing data, and interpreting results. Students also learn to reflect critically on the ethical, intellectual, personal, and civic aspects of their experiences while producing tangible research products (usually reports) for their community partners.

Service-learning has grown in popularity in recent years, and research on service-learning has responded to faculty concerns about academic rigor, assessment, and connections between students' community service in college and later participation in public life. Nevertheless, critiques of service-learning include the following: (1) benefits that favor students and faculty instead of the community; (2) lack of intentionality regarding the community role in decision making, planning, and developing projects; and (3) predominately superficial impacts because of limited time in the community. RSL proponents have taken these partnership critiques seriously, putting greater emphasis on mutual benefits and long-term partnership development. In RSL, students are treated as colleagues, not just volunteers or interns. Likewise, RSL faculty are not just teachers, they are also collaborators and co-learners. Finally, the community is not just a place or a host, but a partner articulating needs and collaborating in developing strategies and setting goals while benefiting from the knowledge-generating mission of the academy.

Designing the Course

Our RSL course, Conservation Biology of the Eno River State Park, is a first-year seminar in the interdisciplinary University Writing Program, but it could also be a biology or environmental science seminar. Courses like this are rarely created by one person, so although it was primarily designed and taught by the first author, a biologist, it was transformed into an RSL course with considerable pedagogical [relating to education] support from the second author, an educator and expert in service-learning.

Our first design step was to determine the course goals. Our primary goal was to increase science literacy, but we also wanted students to understand scientific inquiry, gain critical thinking and writing skills, learn about global and local environmental issues, and develop a sense of environmental stewardship.

The next steps were to identify a community partner and to collaboratively develop a research program. Our partners were the staff at a local state park. Together we discussed projects that would help them better manage park resources and that could realistically be done by 12–24 undergraduates per semester. We selected two projects in each semester, accounting for both seasonal issues and the time and effort needed for research. One fall, for example, we conducted a small-mammal inventory before the first frost and then monitored river-water quality the remainder of the semester. Another semester, we monitored a population of aquatic salamanders that are active in winter, then mapped the distributions of invasive plants after their leaves emerged in early spring.

Third, we designed assignments to accomplish our learning objectives. These included research papers on the value of biodiversity and research proposals related to service projects. To facilitate the goal of environmental awareness and stewardship, students kept weekly journals in which they reflected on their service experience and connected their service with the course content.

The final step in course design was determining the content. Instead of asking "What should we cover?" we asked "What do students need to learn to achieve the course goals?" This approach allowed us to target content that facilitated the development of critical thinking and writing skills and to exclude content that was not strictly relevant.

Students as Colleagues

RSL facilitates student learning in two ways. First, it promotes active learning by inviting students to help set the research agenda and having them participate in every facet of planning and implementing research projects. This collaboration also creates more opportunities for faculty to address students' misconceptions and faulty logic. Students explore topics more deeply and directly experience the complexity, hard work, frustrations, and rewards of doing science. Students also begin to view themselves as budding scientists.

The second way RSL promotes learning is by challenging students to connect the classroom material with meaningful and productive community applications. Real-world problem solving not only increases student interest but also can facilitate deep and sustained learning. Students develop as scientific thinkers through a process of action and reflection described by David Kolb (1981). Students deepen their thinking about conservation biology as they move from concrete experience (fieldwork) to reflective observation (journaling about experiences and receiving feedback from peers) to abstract conceptualization (writing projects that include case study analysis and library research connected to fieldwork) and to active experimentation (research proposals on pressing issues students identify during fieldwork). This process not only exposes students to multiple modes of learning, but it also is recursive [a procedure that can repeat itself indefinitely], allowing students to act, reflect, draw conclusions, and apply what they have learned throughout the semester. . . .

Furthermore, RSL facilitates greater awareness of significant issues within the community and helps build a stronger community through networking and helping students move beyond short-term civic engagement to becoming environmental stewards. Perhaps because of these benefits, we saw increased student engagement. After the semester ended, nearly a third of the 47 students who took this course continued working with community partners through independent studies or paid summer internships.

Faculty as Collaborators

Unquestionably, integrating RSL into non-laboratory-based science courses requires considerably more effort from faculty than traditional lecture-style or seminar courses. If done well, however, this approach integrates teaching with research interests and creates research opportunities for both faculty and students. In fact, when faculty view their teaching responsibilities as complementary to their research interests rather than competing for scarce time, teaching becomes more efficient and enjoyable.

RSL may also make teaching more effective by promoting active learning. Many faculty acknowledge that active learning increases understanding but struggle to implement it. Simply "tacking on" active learning exercises to an existing teaching style may often feel contrived. In RSL, in contrast, active learn-

A Sample of Research Service-Learning Student Evaluations

* The activit[ies] I found most relevant (in this course) were the trips to the Eno River, because the time spent out there is priceless. Getting someone out there and teaching them about nature within that setting is better than any teaching that can be done within the classroom or out of a textbook.

* The service has been lots of fun. It is true that you learn the most when you actually see (science) being done or do it yourself.

* Being able to see both the scientific process in the field as well as the problems that can arise has broadened my view of science in general.

* I find (my research) project particularly inspiring because I know that with some research and hard work, I will have the knowledge and ability to actually implement a program which could really make a difference in the state of the Eno River and . . . in the lives of many local residents.

* This class has shown me that we as students can make a difference in the world, and has provided us the knowledge and path to do so.

Julie A. Reynolds and Jennifer Ahern-Dodson,
"Promoting Science Literacy Through Research
Service-Learning—An Emerging Pedagogy with Significant
Benefits for Students, Faculty, Universities, and Communities,"
Journal of College Science Teaching, *July–August 2010.*

ing is fully integrated into the course and therefore may work more naturally. Additionally, because students and faculty are working together to answer the same scientific questions, faculty can more easily identify essential and nonessential content.

What we did not anticipate were the professional and personal rewards that resulted from creating this course. It catalyzed numerous interdisciplinary collaborations within and beyond our university, with nonacademic scientists, and with members of our community. Consequently, we have contributed to five ongoing research projects, received several grants to continue the research begun in this course, and expanded the project to include Citizen Scientists. Finally, the course allowed us to pursue our interests in community service and meet fellow citizens with similar interests and concerns about our community and the environment.

Communities as Partners

A premise of RSL is that students and faculty collaborate with community partners to identify significant research questions whose answers would benefit the community. Although RSL is applicable to many academic disciplines, it seems especially relevant to the biological and earth sciences because of the urgency of many environmental problems (e.g., global warming, loss of biodiversity) coupled with—typically—insufficient funding to monitor these problems. Thus, RSL not only promotes collaboration but also provides much-needed people power for research projects. In the four semesters this course has been taught, students conducted over 1,400 hours of research in the Eno River State Park. Grants paid for another 1,500 hours of full-time summer research.

Community partners also benefit from the students' new insights and perspectives. We discovered, for example, that partners had better access to unpublished reports and governmental documents, whereas students had better access to peer-reviewed journals. Consequently, information was shared in both directions.

Colleges and universities can benefit from RSL by being visibly more engaged in and with surrounding communities. Institutions are responding to calls to be an "engaged campus," not only to prepare students to be civically responsible, but also to create knowledge with and for their communities. Many institutions, including ours, articulate the goal of civic engagement in strategic plans and mission statements. Engaged campuses are also perceived as good neighbors, particularly if much of the engagement happens in the host city. Local settings, like the Eno River, are easily accessible and cost-effective, and create opportunities for both long-term relationships and multiyear projects. All these factors may enhance the public image of the university as a good citizen. . . .

The Lessons Learned

RSL addresses many of the limitations of traditional service-learning models. First, the approach significantly benefits students and faculty, as well as community partners, colleges, and universities. Communities benefit by collaborating on the research agenda and getting answers to pertinent scientific questions. Colleges and universities benefit by being visibly more engaged with surrounding communities. Student learning is deeper and longer lasting because students are researching authentic scientific questions within their community.

And finally, RSL allows faculty to combine three significant aspects of academic life—teaching, research, and service—in one course, and to share that enriched experience with students and the community. Notably, RSL provides both teaching and research opportunities.

Second, RSL explicitly includes community partners in project development, priority setting, decision making, and planning. This approach debunks the mythical roles of the university as provider of solutions and the community as passive recipient. RSL facilitates faculty and students conducting research with the community, not on the community. Thus, "the community" becomes an authentic partner rather than simply a location in which to conduct research.

Third, RSL inspires students to continue their work beyond a single semester and provides a model for deepening their involvement. Consequently, learning outcomes extend over time and connect to overall student development. This cultivates longer-term relationships between faculty and community partners. By sustaining projects over time, RSL deepens the impacts of the research in the community.

RSL is certainly not without challenges, but we think that the benefits are worth the effort. This approach promotes science literacy by presenting science as a way of thinking rather than as a body of knowledge. Using RSL allowed our students to ask and answer authentic scientific questions and exposed them to the strengths and limitations of the scientific method. Finally, we believe that RSL teaches students to use scientific knowledge and ways of thinking in the service of society.

7

> *"The freedom for our kids to volun-*
> *teer—or not—and to choose where and*
> *how long they volunteer, is . . . vital."*

Mandatory Service Learning Limits Freedom of Choice

Practical Homeschooling

The editors of Practical Homeschooling *maintain in the follow-*
ing viewpoint that there is nothing voluntary about mandatory
voluntary service. Plans to require middle and high school stu-
dents to perform community service at government-approved
volunteer sites in exchange for an educational tax credit are in-
appropriate in challenging economic times. Moreover, the au-
thors argue, calls for a civilian national security force, even
couched in terms of voluntary service, are reminiscent of youth
enlistment programs used by Adolf Hitler. In a free country, the
authors reason, children should be free to choose whether they
want to volunteer.

"Taking Our Kids Hostage: The New Government Order for Mandatory 'Voluntary' Service," *Practical Homeschooling*, March–April 2009. ©2009 Home Life, Inc. Originally published in Practical Homeschooling magazine #87, Mar-Apr 2009, a publication of Home Life, Inc., PO Box 1190, Fenton, MO 63026-1190, (800) 346-6322, www .home-school.com. Used by permission.

As you read, consider the following questions:

1. In the opinion of the editors of *Practical Homeschooling*, what dictator other than Adolf Hitler enlisted young people as enforcers?

2. What two American philosophers invented the concept of service-based learning, according to the authors?

3. What fields of service would be part of the curriculum at the proposed US Public Service Academy?

Above the gates of the Auschwitz concentration camp, where over a million prisoners were killed during World War II, is this motto: "Arbeit Macht Frei." This is German for "Work Makes (You) Free." The illusory promise: Do whatever the government says, no matter how servile, and you will be liberated. The truth: The only "liberation" Germany offered those unfortunate prisoners was death by gassing, starvation, medical experimentation, and overwork.

Concentration camps like Auschwitz were used to house Jews, gypsies, dissenters, and other "un-German" elements. To control the German population itself, Adolf Hitler and his National Socialist German Workers Party (the word "Nazi" comes from "Nationalsozialistische Deutsche Arbeiterpartei") had other tools: a totally compliant media, compromised churches (uncontrolled churches were outlawed), the Gestapo, and of course, the Hitler Youth Brigade.

Using the Young as Enforcers

First established in 1922, enlistment in Hitler Youth became mandatory for all young Germans, with compulsory attendance at all meetings by 1939. For 10- to 18-year-old boys, it started out with enjoyable Boy Scout-like activities, but quickly moved to training in military discipline and tactics. Older boys were encouraged to be cruel to the younger ones, in order to "toughen them up." For girls, it was mainly about becoming physically fit to be good Aryan mothers. Both groups were encouraged to idolize Hitler and support him in every way possible, including informing on "unpatriotic" family members.

Other dictators had their own ways of enlisting young people as enforcers. In China, Communist Party Chairman Mao [Zedong] bypassed the Communist hierarchy and set up his own personality cult, the infamous "Red Guards." These young adults and teens were originally charged with tearing down the "Four Olds" of Chinese society (old customs, old culture, old habits, and old ideas). However, they quickly began denouncing, attacking, and executing people they considered counterrevolutionary.

With this background in mind, those who know history became nervous when, in a July 2, 2008, campaign speech, Democratic [presidential] candidate Barack Obama said, "We cannot continue to rely on our military in order to achieve the national security objectives that we've set. We've got to have a civilian national security force that's just as powerful, just as strong, just as well-funded."

A Civilian National Security Force

The reference to a "civilian national security force" mysteriously was scrubbed from the official transcript of the speech shortly after it was posted, but by then millions had already seen that part of the speech on YouTube, including your editors.

Later that year, Obama's Republican "opponent," Senator John McCain, joined him at the September 11 ServiceNation summit. There, they both helped "kick off the movement to inspire an America in which, by 2020, 100 million citizens will volunteer time in schools, workplaces, and faith-based and community institutions each and every year (up from 61 million today), and that increasing numbers of Americans annually will commit a year of their lives to national service . . . one million Americans a year in full-time service by the year 2020."

Ah, volunteering! That's all the "civilian national security force" lingo was about. Now we can all relax. Not exactly. This won't be your father's volunteering.

Mandatory Voluntary Service

I read about this 15 years or so ago in *Chronicles* magazine. It made such an impression on me at the time that I still remember it.

The topic was "mandatory voluntary service," and if you think that's a contradiction in terms, I couldn't agree with you more.

It all actually started back in the early 1900s, when American philosophers William James and John Dewey (yes, that John Dewey—the fellow who switched American public schools from "education" to "socialization") invented the concept of "service-based learning." In 1910, James wrote a famous essay, "The Moral Equivalence of War," in which he called for national conscription in the cause of vigorously implementing socialist ideals.

World War I and the Great Depression came along and knocked this idea off the front list, but it came surging back in 1993, when President Bill Clinton signed the National and Community Service Trust Act. This created AmeriCorps—a vehicle for paying young people to "volunteer" in government-approved organizations—and the Corporation for National and Community Service—an organization set up like a foundation, to give money to advance the cause of mandatory volunteerism.

After 1993, a number of attempts were made to force mandatory "service" on the American people. Senator [Ernest] Hollings (D-SC) tried and failed to push his Universal National Service Act through in 2003. Congressman [Charles B.]

Rangel (D-NY) introduced his Universal National Service Act in 2006 and 2007. Like most bills, it went nowhere. However, support was growing on both sides of the aisle. Neoconservatives envisioned mandatory service as a way to teach discipline and fair play to ghetto youth in camps far away from their drug-riddled neighborhoods. Liberals loved the idea of getting millions of kids off in camps where they could be indoctrinated in good liberal thinking. However, events such as 9/11 [the September 11, 2001, terrorist attacks] and the Iraq war took center stage, while the political debate centered on issues such as immigration and homosexual rights. There was no time or political energy to push through an unpopular mandatory plan of civilian service.

Things perked up for mandatory national service in 2007. In September . . . of that year, *Time* published an entire issue pushing the idea. Then, in early 2008, the ServiceNation Campaign kicked off. The founders of City Year and the Peace Corps, the first director of AmeriCorps, 106 private organizations, and some well-placed corporate partners, all "spontaneously" decided that now was the time to make their dream of drafting all American kids—and eventually, everyone else as well—a reality. That's when both presidential candidates, one of whom was bound to get elected, joined in.

Obama Will Require Students to Work

In a February 3, 2008, speech at UCLA [University of California, Los Angeles], Michelle Obama said:

> Barack Obama will require you to work. He is going to demand that you shed your cynicism. That you put down your divisions. That you come out of your isolation, that you move out of your comfort zones. That you push yourselves to be better. And that you engage. Barack will never allow you to go back to your lives as usual, uninvolved, uninformed.

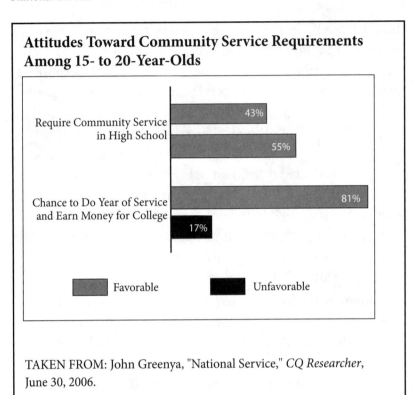

Attitudes Toward Community Service Requirements Among 15- to 20-Year-Olds

Require Community Service in High School
- 43%
- 55%

Chance to Do Year of Service and Earn Money for College
- 81%
- 17%

Favorable   Unfavorable

TAKEN FROM: John Greenya, "National Service," *CQ Researcher*, June 30, 2006.

Mere over-the-top political-speak? Not so. Below is what the original "America Serves" page on Obama's official "President-Elect" transition website, change.gov, used to say. (After a number of bloggers and speakers commented on it, the page was changed to remove the word "required," which has been highlighted in the direct quote below from the original page).

The Obama administration will call on Americans to serve in order to meet the nation's challenges. President-Elect Obama will expand national service programs like Ameri-Corps and Peace Corps and will create a new Classroom Corps to help teachers in underserved schools, as well as a new Health Corps, Clean Energy Corps, and Veterans Corps. Obama will call on citizens of all ages to serve America, by developing a plan to *require* 50 hours of community service in middle school and high school and 100 hours of community service in college every year. Obama will encourage retiring Americans to serve by improving programs available for individuals over age 55, while at the same time promoting youth programs such as YouthBuild and Head Start.

That went over like a lead balloon, so a carrot was added in place of the too-obvious stick. Here's what the updated page currently says: Obama and Biden will call on citizens of all ages to serve. They'll set a goal that all middle school and high school students engage in 50 hours of community service a year, and develop a plan for all college students who engage in 100 hours of community service to receive a fully refundable tax credit of $4,000 for their education.

Great! Since our economy is doing so well, let's dish out $4K per student for "volunteering." But at approved volunteer sites only, of course. . . .

Well-Indoctrinated Leaders

This is already being implemented. The "GIVE Act," H.R. 1388 [renamed the Edward M. Kennedy Serve America Act], was signed into law on April 21. It massively expands and funds the [Corporation for National and Community Service], in a bid to "manage" up to 8 or 9 million "volunteers." H.R. 1444, the "SERVE Act," also establishes a Congressional Commission on Civic Service, among whose tasks are figuring out "whether a workable, fair and reasonable mandatory service requirement for all able young people could be developed, and how such a requirement could be implemented . . ." [H.R. 1444 did not become law.]

Now comes the "Tuition-Free Public Service Academy Bill" [H.R. 2102] sponsored by Rep. Jim Moran, D-VA. In his own words, it would create a new four-year academy "modeled after the current military service academies at West Point, Annapolis and Colorado Springs." The idea? To "cultivate and groom a new generation of young leaders dedicated to public service. The Public Service Academy would offer four years of tuition-free education in exchange for five years of civilian service following graduation. Eligible fields of service would include public education, public health, law enforcement and government."

Since four-year colleges already offer degrees in public education, public health, law enforcement, and government, we have to wonder why a special quasi-military academy is needed for this. Unless the goal is to force every kid, and eventually everyone of all ages, to "volunteer." Then it will certainly help to have well-indoctrinated "leaders" for the "volunteers."

The freedom for our kids to volunteer—or not—and to choose where and how long they volunteer, is as vital as the freedom to homeschool.

We've won other political battles; God willing, we'll win this one, too.

Let "Freedom of Choice in Volunteering" become our watchword. It sure beats "Arbeit Macht Frei."

Periodical Bibliography

The following articles have been selected to supplement the diverse views presented in this chapter.

Sean Creighton	"Significant Findings in Campus-Community Engagement: Community Partner Perspective," *Journal for Civic Commitment*, 2008.
Candace de Russy	"Obama's Corrosive Communitarian 'Service' for Students," *Pajamas Media*, December 4, 2008. http://pajamasmedia.com.
Kathy R. Fox	"Children Making a Difference: Developing Awareness of Poverty Through Service Learning," *Social Studies*, December 2009.
Andrew Furco and Susan Root	"Research Demonstrates the Value of Service Learning," *Phi Delta Kappan*, February 2010.
James C. Kielsmeier	"Build a Bridge Between Service and Learning," *Phi Delta Kappan*, February 2010.
Kathleen Kennedy Manzo	"Service Learning; Engaged for Success: Service-Learning as a Tool for High School-Dropout Prevention," *Education Week*, April 23, 2008.
Kathy Payne and Betty Edwards	"Service Learning Enhances Education for Young Adolescents," *Phi Delta Kappan*, February 2010.
Deborah Perkins-Gough	"Can Service Learning Keep Students in School?" *Educational Leadership*, May 2009.
Cynthia Sims	"Service-Learning Mentoring for High School Transition and Student Leadership," *Techniques*, April 2010.
Lawrence Wood	"Bridge Work," *Christian Century*, February 23, 2010.

OPPOSING
VIEWPOINTS®
SERIES

CHAPTER 4

What Role Should the Government Play in National Service?

Chapter Preface

While Americans generally place a high value on serving others in need, commentators fiercely debate the government's role in such efforts, as can be seen in the viewpoints of the authors in the following chapter. While the idea of national service is not new, following the terrorist attacks of September 11, 2001, and the devastation of Hurricane Katrina in 2005, calls for all Americans to in some way serve their communities have grown in fervor. In his January 2002 State of the Union address, President George W. Bush asked Americans to give four thousand hours over their lifetimes to serve their communities. Following his inauguration in 2009, President Barack Obama made similar calls. His use of the word *universal*, however, prompted many commentators to express concern that his objective was to make national service compulsory. Indeed, one of the most controversial national service debates is whether service should be mandatory. While some claim that all Americans should be required to serve the nation in some way, others believe that service should always be voluntary.

Opponents argue that mandated service is not true service. People should perform good works only because they choose to, these analysts assert. Moreover, they maintain, any government program that pays people to perform good deeds is not only costly but also inappropriate. James Bovard, president and founder of the free market think tank the Competitive Enterprise Institute, considers mandatory national service programs a boondoggle—unnecessary, impractical, and wasteful. "It will always be a boondoggle when you are rounding up people and paying them for doing good deeds,"[1] he claims. Bruce Chapman, founder and codirector of the Discovery In-

1. Quoted in Kelly Beaucar Vlahos, "AmeriCorps on the Chopping Block," Fox News, March 20, 2006.

stitute, agrees. "Indeed, when coercion or inducements are provided, as in the various national service schemes, the spirit of service is to that degree corrupted,"[2] he reasons. "Enrollment in a government-funded self-improvement project or acceptance of a government job [cannot] be called true service," he concludes.

Those who support mandatory national service counter that being paid for service does not diminish its value. Military service, they reason, is no less a civic sacrifice because soldiers are paid. Americans who do not choose to serve in the military should be required to give something back for the rights and benefits of citizenship and be paid for their service, supporters claim. Gary L. Yates, president and chief executive officer of the California Wellness Foundation, asserts, "Mandatory national service would provide a way for the youth of this nation to give something back for the freedoms they enjoy and to work side by side with other young Americans for a common national purpose."[3] Many young people agree. In response to claims that the government has no right to demand service from young Americans, Vanderbilt University student Sean Harris counters, "In my opinion, the government does have that right and should exercise it. As citizens of the U.S., we enjoy the protection of American law and the shelter of the American government. In return for this protection all citizens owe this country any service it requests, so long as that service is meaningful."[4]

Mandatory national service remains controversial. The authors in the following chapter debate similar issues concerning the role government should play in national service. Whatever that role, few deny the value of America's youth as social capital. Steven A. Culbertson, chief executive officer of Youth Ser-

2. Quoted in John Greenya, "National Service," *CQ Researcher*, June 30, 2006.
3. Gary L. Yates, *California Wellness Foundation News*, February 1, 2002.
4. Sean M. Harris, "Serving Up a Different System," *Current*, December 5, 2005.

vice America, maintains, "Young people are powerful change makers around the world. They possess the energy and ingenuity to help tackle the world's most complex problems, which makes them assets and resources for our communities."[5] Whether the use of this social capital will be mandated or remain voluntary remains to be seen.

5. Quoted in "Young People Around the World Stand Up and Take Action for the 7th Annual Global Youth Service Day," Youth Service America, April 2006. www.ysa.org.

| "We need to maximize the impact of national service through strategic investments in existing nonprofit organizations and by funding social entrepreneurs."

The Government Should Support National Service

Shirley Sagawa

In the following viewpoint, Shirley Sagawa argues that national service programs have proven that they meet the needs of American communities. Thus, she asserts, the federal government should reauthorize and increase support for these programs. Based on decades of experience, the federal government can narrow the role of national service programs, making it easier to address America's pressing social problems, Sagawa claims. Moreover, she maintains, the government should take advantage of program alumni and add innovative new programs to improve life for all Americans. Sagawa, the first managing director of the Corporation for National and Community Service, is a scholar at the Center for American Progress, a liberal think tank.

Shirley Sagawa, "Introduction and Summary," *Serving America: A National Service Agenda for the Next Decade*. Center for American Progress, September 2007. This material was created by the Center for American Progress. www.americanprogress.org.

As you read, consider the following questions:

1. According to Sagawa, what criticism have conservatives used to deride national service programs?

2. What percentage of Community HealthCorps members enter the health care field after their service, in the author's view?

3. What does the author suggest are ways to expand national service opportunities during key life transitions?

There is strong evidence over the past eight decades that national service plays an effective role in solving specific problems in every sector of our society. In the 1930s, the Depression-era Civilian Conservation Corps started by President Franklin Roosevelt engaged 3 million unemployed young men to fight soil erosion by planting trees, building structures in national parks, and otherwise protecting America's natural resources. VISTA [Volunteers in Service to America] volunteers working to alleviate poverty in the 1960s paved the way for national service programs dedicated to helping our senior citizens in the 1970s. Youth service in the 1980s led to the creation and a full range of national service programs that engaged American youth and adults, including the Points of Light Foundation, in the early 1990s.

Responding to Opposition

Then, in 1993, President Clinton proposed the AmeriCorps program, building on the national service demonstration program enacted by Congress three years earlier, and extending and expanding other service programs already in operation. Unfortunately, America's progressive experiment with national service legislation ran into concerted conservative opposition. Some conservatives derided these programs, arguing that they simply paid people to volunteer. Authorizing legislation enacted in 1993 expired in 1997, the victim of calculated neglect by the congressional opponents.

And yet individual members of Congress, recognizing the important role of national service in our public life, came together in an informal bipartisan coalition to continue funding these programs, enabling millions of Americans—including half a million AmeriCorps members—to demonstrate the effectiveness of national service. AmeriCorps members served their communities through programs supported in whole or in part by this legislation, with additional funding from private funders, as well as state and local governments.

Innovative Initiatives

The flexible and community-driven nature of these service programs resulted in a diversity of innovative initiatives, continuing this great experiment in national service despite the absence of authorizing legislation from Congress. Organizations ranging from local schools and after-school programs to large national youth corps and brand-name nonprofits took part. Social entrepreneurs, in particular, looked to national service to provide the human and financial resources they needed to grow their new and creative social service organizations.

In some cases, the availability of federal funds inspired issue-focused organizations to incorporate service into their delivery mechanisms. In other cases, funded nonprofit organizations considered national service as their primary mission. In still other cases, organizations looked to AmeriCorps members to create an infrastructure for engaging volunteers.

While not every program met its objectives, many did. Numerous evaluations and studies have documented the results of service programs, and experience has provided insights into what works for different situations. Today, national service programs that tackle a range of pressing issues—from global warming and economic self-sufficiency to community health and quality education—provide a unique support system for communities and have a proven track record of improving society as a whole. . . .

Programs That Work

A range of . . . programs . . . work, among them:

- AmeriCorps members have dramatically expanded the capacity of Habitat for Humanity to increase its output of volunteer-built homes.

- EducationWorks AmeriCorps members provide clubs, summer camps, and youth leadership programs through urban schools, increasing school attendance by an average of 20 days and improving students' academic achievement and behavior.

- Eighty-five percent of Community HealthCorps members opt to enter the health care field after their term of service, which they spend enrolling patients into free or low-cost health insurance plans, learning to manage chronic conditions, and helping them navigate through the health care system.

The success of these and other national service programs is precisely why congressional reauthorization of these programs is long overdue.

Economic and Societal Potential

Partisan and ideological conflict over the past decade has prevented a constructive reexamination of national service's even greater economic and societal potential. Cases in point:

- Expanded national service programs dedicated to providing educational help to our youth and to adults seeking new educational or employment opportunities would boost our national economic competitiveness and enhance social mobility.

Strong Momentum for Citizen Service

- Last year, 62 million Americans gave 8 billion hours of service to our nation.

- The number of AmeriCorps applications has shot up, . . . and volunteer centers and nonprofits are reporting increases in volunteers.

- Millennials are volunteering more than past generations while [baby] boomers will dramatically boost the number of older adult volunteers in the coming decades.

- Leaders in every sector—from corporate CEOs [chief executive officers] and college presidents to governors and grant makers—recognize that service is a proven strategy to tackle tough challenges.

- Social entrepreneurs are redefining service and volunteering, and Web 2.0 technologies are providing new ways for citizens to engage and connect.

Statement of Stephen Goldsmith
Before the Senate Committee on Health, Education, Labor
and Pensions on the Next Generation of National Service,
March 10, 2009.

- Growth of national service programs in the health care arena could help provide greater economic security to the millions of Americans unable to access decent health insurance.

- New national service programs designed to lead our nation toward a low-carbon economy in communities across the country would help our nation confront the threat of global warming.

- New and existing national service programs can increase upward social mobility by connecting disadvantaged and disconnected youth with school and work through programs that combine opportunities to participate in service with training in fields that are in high demand.

- National service programs can accelerate innovation in the social services sector by providing human resources to social entrepreneurs.

Sharpening the Role of National Service

It is time to make use of the experience gained over the past decades to sharpen the role of national service and transform these programs into large-scale efforts to solve some of America's most pressing problems. Today we as a nation are unable to realize the full potential of national service programs. We need to maximize the impact of national service through strategic investments in existing nonprofit organizations and by funding social entrepreneurs. Specifically, to give national service the attention it so clearly deserves, the Center for American Progress offers a comprehensive set of recommendations, among them:

- Create *growth funds* to expand highly effective national service programs meeting specific priority needs, including youth and adult education, community health, alternative energy opportunities, and economic and social mobility.

- Substantially increase the funds available for planning grants and innovative new programs by creating a national service *Innovation Fund* to test other ways that national service can address priority issues, such as teaching immigrants English, closing the digital divide, and ending rural poverty.

Expand specific national service opportunities for Americans during key life transitions, including:

- A *Summer of Service* for middle schoolers in transition to high school;

- *Youth Corps* to engage disconnected youth in service while they work on their GEDs [General Educational Development] and learn job skills;

- Opportunities to attract *recent college graduates* into social service fields through full-time AmeriCorps service;

- Engaging *retiring adults* and adults in career transitions in teaching, mentoring, and learning opportunities through national service.

Amplify the long-term impact of national service by:

- Investing in *social entrepreneurship* by helping Ameri-Corps alumni create new social service programs.

- Mobilizing *AmeriCorps alumni as a "ready reserve"* to provide skills useful in times of crisis and as a resource to address ongoing challenges faced by communities everywhere.

- Investing in *nonprofit capacity building* by continuing to allow AmeriCorps and AmeriCorps VISTA members to make nonprofit capacity building their primary activity.

- *Expanding private sector investment in national service* by increasing the availability of and ease of applying for cost-sharing and education-award-only programs.

In these many ways, national service can be used as an innovative platform for change, improving quality of life for all citizens.

| *"Any program of universal national service is unconstitutional and un-American."*

Government-Sponsored Universal National Service Is Un-American

Patrick Krey

The concept of universal national service runs counter to the right of all Americans to decide when and how they want to serve their communities, asserts Patrick Krey in the following viewpoint. Mandatory service is a form of involuntary servitude, and imposing taxes to serve state-sponsored goals is un-American, he maintains. In truth, Krey claims, past national service programs have been poorly managed and are wasteful. Unfortunately, universal national service threatens to reduce the impact of private charities by attaching financial strings that hinder innovative programs, he argues. Krey is a lawyer and writer from New York.

As you read, consider the following questions:

1. According to French economist Frédéric Bastiat, what are the two types of effects produced by laws?

Patrick Krey, "Any Volunteers for National Service?" *New American*, vol. 25, February 2, 2009, p. 10. Reproduced by permission.

2. From where does Krey claim the money for spending on national service programs will come?

3. In the author's view, what might the impact of mandating volunteerism at an early age have on future community service?

National service is often associated with patriotism, but the degree to which it becomes compulsory is the same degree to which it becomes involuntary servitude.

Proponents of universal national service claim that it will bring this nation together and teach younger generations about what it means to be an American. Sadly, many Americans seem to believe those claims. Even with information that the program will be virtually mandatory and might lead to a new version of the draft, some Americans might shrug their shoulders and say "so what?" Well, there is much more wrong with national service than is immediately apparent.

Nineteenth-century French economist and statesman Frédéric Bastiat famously wrote in his essay "What Is Seen and What Is Not Seen" that "a law produces not only one effect, but a series of effects. Of these effects, the first alone is immediate; it appears simultaneously with its cause; it is seen. The other effects emerge only subsequently; they are not seen; we are fortunate if we foresee them." What other effects could there be to this universal national service?

Another Big-Government Program

National service is just another costly and wasteful big-government program. Like most federal government programs, it will be top-heavy, slow reacting, expensive, ineffective, and administered from [Washington,] D.C. To get a good idea of what these new "corps" will be doing, one only has to review what AmeriCorps has been up to since its inception. Author James Bovard has documented the almost comical "volunteerism" that AmeriCorps has produced:

In most areas of AmeriCorps activity, its effect is negligible—at best: ... An AmeriCorps member helped organize a "Pink Prom," the first gay youth dance in Snohomish County, Washington. AmeriCorps members in Worcester, Massachusetts, presented lessons in half a dozen schools about "Super Bowl Surge"—the problems that occur when millions of people watching the big game use the bathroom during halftime. ... Puppet shows are a favorite activity for AmeriCorps members. In Springfield, Illinois, AmeriCorps members presented a puppet show to edify three-year-olds at the Little Angels Child Care Center by alerting them to the benefits of smoke detectors.

Bovard also explains that AmeriCorps is grossly mismanaged and has yet to produce any serious, tangible results.

Though AmeriCorps abounds in "feel-good" projects, it has never provided credible evidence of benefit to the United States. The Office of Management and Budget [OMB] concluded in 2003 that "AmeriCorps has not been able to demonstrate results. Its current focus is on the amount of time a person serves, as opposed to the impact on the community or participants." OMB noted in 2004, "AmeriCorps accomplishments are difficult to measure, but its reported impact is small." The General Accounting Office [GAO] noted in 2000 that AmeriCorps "generally reports the results of its programs and activities by quantifying the amount of services AmeriCorps participants perform." GAO criticized AmeriCorps for failing to make any effort to measure the actual effect of its members' actions.

Creating More Taxes and Inflation

What will happen when taxes are raised to pay for this increased spending? The money will have to come from somewhere. It will either be raised by taxes or created by the Federal Reserve, thereby inflating the money supply. Either way, the American people will bear the brunt of the cost. How will this increased spending impact present levels of volunteerism and charitable giving? There is the real threat of crowding out private sector charity by having the federal government take such a large leap into bureaucratizing community service. Jim Grichar, a former economist for the federal government, wrote that "real volunteerism in this country still exists, and if taxpayers were not being mulcted [punished by a fine] for every goofy and evil social welfare scheme, they would have the time and resources to devote to increased genuine charitable efforts." Grichar, having witnessed AmeriCorps firsthand, also wrote that "the real horror is always the same—you as a taxpayer pay more and get less than you would have if the private sector—either for-profit businesses or nongovernment-funded private charities—handled the problem. The inefficiency, waste, fraud, other corruption and abuse inflicted on taxpayers by the federal government—like all governments, it has a territorial monopoly of power and the authority to tax citizens to pay for its activities—appears endless, a price we have to pay for progress."

Destroying Private Charity

Research has shown that believers in big government do not put much stock in private charity. Syracuse University Professor Arthur Brooks, author of *Who Really Cares*, did research to see who gives more to charity between liberals and conservatives. "When you look at the data, it turns out the conservatives give about 30 percent more. And incidentally, conservative-headed families make slightly less money. . . . *You find that people who believe it's the government's job to make incomes more equal, are far less likely to give their money away.*" (Emphasis added.) If those trends continue, this huge national-service initiative could have a similar effect. People who volunteer through government programs will forgo volunteering through private organizations. As more people believe that charity is the responsibility of government, private charity and willful volunteerism will decline.

176

In addition, by mandating volunteerism at such an early age, universal national service might have the effect of discouraging future community service. According to a research article published in [a] journal of the American Psychological Society, "Students who are not willing or not ready to volunteer—but who are required to by their school—may be less likely to volunteer again in the future."

The reality is that present government policies are obstacles to private volunteerism. Former special assistant to the [Ronald] Reagan administration Doug Bandow, in testimony to Congress on national-service programs, said that while much "worthwhile service work remains to be done across the country . . . government often stands in the way of private individuals and groups who want to help. Such barriers should be stripped away, yet [federal national-service programs] may divert attention from the ways the government hinders private provision of important social services. . . . Restrictions on paratransit operations limit private transportation for the disabled. Regulations also harm other forms of volunteerism. Health regulations prevent restaurants in Los Angeles and elsewhere from donating food to the hungry, for instance. In short, in many cases important needs are unmet precisely because of perverse government policy."

A "Strings Attached" Approach

There is another danger posed by bureaucratizing roles typically run by private churches. [Barack] Obama has vowed to continue George W. Bush's faith-based initiatives, but he wants to put his own mark on it: "Make no mistake, as someone who used to teach constitutional law, I believe deeply in the separation of church and state, but I don't believe this partnership will endanger that idea—so long as we follow a few basic principles. . . . First, if you get a federal grant, you can't use that grant money to proselytize to the people you help and you can't discriminate against them—or against the people you hire—on the basis of their religion. Second, federal dollars that go directly to churches, temples, and mosques can only be used on secular programs. And we'll also ensure that taxpayer dollars only go to those programs that actually work."

Basically, this is more of the "strings attached" federal funding approach. Obama will be all too willing to throw federal funds around for national-service programs, even ones that are involved with religious charities, but participating religious charities will have to abide by the rules of the secular state. One can only imagine what will happen to volunteer work for such controversial issues as abortion or sex education. If a church doesn't follow Washington's direction in controversial areas, they run the risk of being left behind in the national-service tidal wave of state-controlled "volunteers."

A Form of Indoctrination

Federally funded and directed programs would be a great way for establishment leaders to control the debate on the issues. Since the 1950s, the federal government has become more and more involved in education. During this time, education policy has become more propagandized and directed from Washington. Jacob Hornberger, president of the Future of Freedom Foundation, writes that "public schooling has achieved success in one important area: the creation of a flock of good little citizens who believe that the paternalistic welfare state constitutes freedom and free enterprise. Indeed, herein lies the power of public schooling—the power of government employees to indoctrinate children, year after year, with their officially approved version of what it means to be free." Could national-service programs be another method employed by the government to "indoctrinate" our nation's youth? The possibility is certainly there.

The "ClassroomCorps" could assist with teaching children the accepted progressive notions of the day. The "Health-

Corps" would immediately put to work a new coalition clamoring for socialized medicine and further government intervention into health care. The "Clean Energy Corps" could spread the message of a "necessary" global solution to the dire threat of "climate change" most likely administered through the UN [United Nations]. Finally, the "Homeland Security Corps" could help train a generation of citizens on how to implement the directives of the federal government at a moment's notice. What starts out as voluntary soon becomes mandatory. This initiative would also assist with the continued centralization of power in Washington. In every way, national service would only serve to tie our nation's youth more closely to government and indoctrinate them in the mindless worship of the all-powerful State as the solution to all of life's problems. This new "service" generation would be more willing to accept big-government solutions at both the national and global level.

An Un-American and Unconstitutional Program

The whole notion of universal national service runs counter to the founding principles of our nation. Alex Epstein, writing in the online *Capitalism Magazine*, explains that "America was founded on the principle of individualism: the idea that each individual is a sovereign being with the moral right to his own life and to the achievement of his own goals. This is the basis of the political idea, enshrined in our Declaration of Independence, that the individual possesses inalienable rights to life, liberty, and the pursuit of happiness. The Founders accordingly reconceived the purpose of government as being the servant of the individual, rather than his master. . . . This collectivist belief in the supremacy of the group over the individual is the foundation of the national-service ideology, which regards the individual as a servant to the nation. The notion that people are 'nothing without the group' and owe their lives—or any portion of them—to the state is antithetical to American individualism and freedom."

Volunteerism as it exists in a free society has virtually nothing in common with the vision of national service promoted by Obama. Sheldon Richman, editor of the *Freeman*, explains that "if people wish to perform service for others, they of course should be free to do so, with their own time and money. They should neither be forced nor use force in the name of service. A legally enforceable obligation to perform service clashes with the principles of the free society and proclaims that individuals are not self-owners but rather the property of society or the state. If there is no right to live for one's own sake, there are no rights at all." Richman also asks, "Where do people get the idea that the Nation is something to be served? . . . This is a profoundly un-American concept. It's far more consistent with the European despotism of the first half of the twentieth century. You don't have to look hard to find quotations by [Benito] Mussolini [fascist dictator of Italy during World War II] (dare I mention [Adolf] Hitler?) about the duty of the individual to serve the Nation. . . . This is not what most Americans thought at the time of the founding."

An End-Run Around the Constitution

The first thing that comes to a constitutionalist's mind after contemplating Obama's proposal is that there is no authorization for it in the Constitution. It appears that Obama hopes to do an end-run around the Constitution by employing the liberally interpreted "General Welfare" clause that is used to justify the taxing and spending powers of Congress. Even with this dubious rationale, the question remains whether universal national service violates the 13th Amendment's prohibition on "involuntary servitude." Ilya Somin, a law professor at George Mason University, certainly thinks so. "I think that the answer is pretty clearly 'yes,' at least if you take the text of the Constitution seriously. . . . Note that the Amendment forbids not only 'slavery' but also 'involuntary servitude,' a provision deliberately inserted to prevent state governments from, in effect, reenslaving blacks by imposing 'temporary' forced labor systems. Mandatory national service, which would require young people to do government-mandated work . . . is pretty clearly involuntary servitude under any reasonable definition of the word."

The truth of the matter is that any program of universal national service is unconstitutional and un-American. Congressman Ron Paul (R-Texas) put it best when he said, "Some politicians simply love the thought of mandatory service to the federal government. . . . Both sides share the same belief that citizens should serve the needs of the state—a belief our founders clearly rejected in the Declaration of Independence. To many politicians, the American government is America. . . . Compulsory national service, whether in the form of military conscription or make-work programs like AmeriCorps, still sells on Capitol Hill. Conscription is wrongly associated with patriotism, when really it represents collectivism and involuntary servitude."

> *"Taxpayers GIVE their money to SERVE a big government agenda under the guise of helping their fellow man. It's charity at the point of a gun."*

Government Funding of National Service Threatens American Freedom

Michelle Malkin

Federally funded national service programs pose a threat to American freedoms, argues Michelle Malkin in the following viewpoint. While few dispute the value of volunteerism, spending taxpayer money to create armies of volunteers to promote a radical liberal social agenda is disturbing, she asserts. Even more troubling, especially for American parents, are efforts to promote a mandatory service requirement for young people, Malkin maintains. Funding costly national service programs to serve political ends is coercive: Charity should be by choice, she claims. Malkin writes conservative commentary for newspapers and magazines nationwide.

Michelle Malkin, "To Give and to Serve: The $6 Billion National Service Boondoggle," *Creators Syndicate*, 2009. Reproduced by permission of Michelle Malkin and Creators Syndicate.

As you read, consider the following questions:

1. In Malkin's opinion, what are volunteerism packages before Congress really about?

2. In what way are those who have watched AmeriCorps from its inception familiar with how these programs have been used, in the author's view?

3. According to the author, what did Representative Virginia Foxx successfully attach to the GIVE Act?

M aybe it's just me, but I find federal legislation titled "The GIVE Act" and "The SERVE Act" downright creepy. Even more troubling: The $6 billion price tag on these bipartisan bills to expand government-funded national service efforts. Volunteerism is a wonderful thing, which is why millions of Americans do it every day without a cent of taxpayer money. But the volunteerism packages on the Hill are less about promoting effective charity than about creating make-work, permanent bureaucracies, and left-wing slush funds.

The House passed the "Generations Invigorating Volunteerism and Education Act"—or the GIVE Act [renamed the Edward M. Kennedy Serve America Act]—last week. The Senate took up the companion "SERVE Act" Tuesday afternoon [February 9, 2010]. According to a Congressional Budget Office analysis of the Senate bill, S. 277, the bill would cost "$418 million in 2010 and about $5.7 billion over the 2010–2014 period." And like most federal programs, these would be sure to grow over time. The bills reauthorize the [Bill] Clinton-era AmeriCorps boondoggle program and an older law, the Domestic Volunteer Service Act of 1973.

Creating New Little Armies

The programs have already been allocated $1.1 billion for fiscal 2009, including $200 million from the porkulus package signed into law last month. In addition to recruiting up to

250,000 enrollees in AmeriCorps, the GIVE/SERVE bills would create new little armies of government volunteers, including a Clean Energy Corps, Education Corps, Healthy Futures Corps, Veterans Service Corps, and an expanded National Civilian Community Corps for disaster relief and energy conservation. And that's not all. Spending would include new funds for:

- Foster Grandparent Program ($115 million);

- Learn and Serve America ($97 million);

- Retired and Senior Volunteer Program ($70 million);

- Senior Companion Program ($55 million);

- $12 million for each of fiscal years 2010 through 2014 for "the Silver Scholarships and Encore Fellowships programs";

- $10 million a year from 2010–2014 for a new "Volunteers for Prosperity" program at USAID to "award grants to fund opportunities for volunteering internationally in coordination with eligible organizations; and

- Social Innovation Fund and Volunteer Generation Fund—$50 million in 2010; $60 million in 2011; $70 million in 2012; $80 million in 2013; and $100 million in 2014.

"Social Innovation Fund?" If that sounds familiar, it should. I reported last fall on the Democratic Party platform's push to fund a "Social Investment Fund Network" that would reward "social entrepreneurs and leading nonprofit organizations" and "support results-oriented innovators." It is essentially a special taxpayer-funded pipeline for radical liberal groups backed by billionaire George Soros that masquerade as public-interest do-gooders.

Especially troublesome to parents' groups concerned about compulsory volunteerism requirements is a provision in the House version, directing Congress to explore "whether a work-

Removing Freedom of Choice

Problem number one with grand schemes for universal voluntary public service is that they can't be both universal and voluntary. If everybody has to do it, then it's not voluntary, is it? And if it's truly up to the individual, then it won't be universal. What advocates of this sort of thing generally have in mind is using the pressures of social conformity and the powers of the state indirectly to remove as much freedom of choice as possible.

Michael Kinsley,
"National Service? Puh-lease,"
Time, *August 30, 2007.*

able, fair, and reasonable mandatory service requirement for all able young people could be developed, and how such a requirement could be implemented in a manner that would strengthen the social fabric of the Nation and overcome civic challenges by bringing together people from diverse economic, ethnic, and educational backgrounds."

Using Programs for Political Purposes

Those who have watched AmeriCorps from its inception are all too familiar with how government voluntarism programs have been used for propaganda and political purposes. AmeriCorps "volunteers" have been put to work lobbying against the voter-approved three-strikes anticrime initiative in California and protesting Republican political events while working for the already heavily-tax-subsidized liberal advocacy group ACORN [Association of Community Organizations for Reform Now].

Citizens Against Government Waste, the D.C. watchdog, also documented national service volunteers lobbying for rent control, expanded federal housing subsidies, and enrollment of more women in the Women, Infants, and Children welfare program. AmeriCorps volunteers have also been paid to shuffle paper at the Department of Justice, the Department of the Interior, the Environmental Protection Agency, the Legal Services Corporation, and the National Endowment for the Arts.

(Now, imagine Obama's troops being sent overseas—out of sight and unaccountable—as part of that $10 million a year USAID/"Volunteers for Prosperity" program. Egad.)

One vigilant House member, GOP Rep. Virginia Foxx, successfully attached an amendment to the GIVE Act to bar national service recipients from engaging in political lobbying, endorsing or opposing legislation, organizing petitions, protests, boycotts, or strikes; providing or promoting abortions or referrals; or influencing union organizing.

Supporters of GIVE/SERVE are now fighting those restrictions tooth and nail, screaming censorship and demanding that the provisions be dropped. Which tells you everything you need to know about the true nature of this boondoggle: Taxpayers GIVE their money to SERVE a big government agenda under the guise of helping their fellow man. It's charity at the point of a gun.

Don't know why, but the creepy title of the Senate bill reminds me of that classic *Twilight Zone* episode, "To Serve Man."[1] Remember?

---

1. The *Twilight Zone* episode to which the author refers concludes with the realization by the episode's human protagonist that the visiting outer space alien's book *To Serve Man* is not a book about how to help humankind but is a cookbook.

> "It's difficult to find anything very sinister in an act that is intended to 'reauthorize and reform' already existing service laws."

Government Funding of National Service Does Not Threaten American Freedom

Fiona Bruce

Fiona Bruce claims in the following viewpoint that the GIVE Act (renamed the Edward M. Kennedy Serve America Act) is not a threat to American freedom—the act simply reauthorizes and reforms national service laws. Nor does the law hide a socialist or fascist agenda to force young people to volunteer, she asserts. Indeed, paying people to provide valuable services to American communities at a nominal cost to taxpayers is a good way to spend American tax dollars, Bruce reasons. Offering diverse students equal access to financial and educational opportunities has long been a goal of government and private institutions, she concludes. Bruce is publicist for the Women's Resource Center at Portland State University.

Fiona Bruce, "Defending Volunteerism," *Daily Vanguard* [Portland State University, OR], April 21, 2009. Copyright ©2009 Portland State University Student Publications. Reproduced by permission.

As you read, consider the following questions:

1. What does GIVE Act funding provide, in Bruce's view?

2. According to the author, what agenda becomes evident in the editorial article to which she is responding?

3. Why was the author surprised to hear that AmeriCorps is a waste of money?

Earlier this month, in the April 7 [2009] issue of the *Vanguard* [a student-run newspaper of Portland State University], an article appeared condemning the recently passed U.S. House Bill 1388—alternately known as the "Generations Invigorating Volunteerism and Education Act," (or G.I.V.E.), aka the Edward M. Kennedy Serve America Act.

The article provided such a litany of (not necessarily related) indignation at the idea of federally funded service learning, as well as some exaggerations of the bill's purpose and outcome, I felt compelled to come to the defense of the GIVE Act, even though that meant reading through the entire bill several times.

Finding Nothing Sinister

It's difficult to find anything very sinister in an act that is intended to "reauthorize and reform" already existing service laws. For example, this bill provides funding to increase the number of positions available to learn-and-serve programs like AmeriCorps, and it also provides minimal stipends for volunteers to groups that benefit seniors, veterans and other underserved or minority populations.

It's basically like a supplement to the limited work-study funds that are also available through the federal government. The act provides more opportunity for people to (voluntarily) participate in service learning.

I imagine that there is potential fault to be found within any piece of legislation, particularly if you want to find fault with it. Andrew Geist, the author of the aforementioned article ["GIVE back"], seems to have wanted very much to find fault with the bill and he succeeds beyond any reasonable expectation.

To be fair, Geist brings up some points well worth consideration, even for those who may not share his views—most notably, he raises the alarm about the section in the bill that calls for the formation of an exploratory committee to study ". . . whether a workable, fair and reasonable mandatory service requirement for all able young people could be developed."

Keep in mind, this is a study. I'm not alarmed by feasibility studies—they are not any guarantee that action will be taken now or later. I do think we should all be aware that there is a possibility that college-aged students might, in exchange for a term of civil service, be provided with a living wage and funds to help pay for their education.

A Positive Thing

I tend to think that this would be a positive thing, both for students and the national and local communities served. The article's author compares this concept—unfavorably—to the draft. He seems to think that mandatory military service is a reasonable expectation but that any service not spent in the military defense of national interests is some sort of moral lapse, as well as a guarantee of economic collapse.

The GIVE Act also makes mention of studying the feasibility of creating national service programs to provide more options for ". . . workers and communities that have been adversely affected by plant closings and job losses," and to the creation of scholarships for people over 55 who have volunteered over 500 hours in service of "areas of national need." Should Geist's argument extend to state that these people should also be drafted to fight in wartime, since they've lost their jobs or are trying to find ways to stay engaged and productive after retirement?

There is terminology in the GIVE Act that encourages what Geist calls "a large social experiment in forced diversity," or, from a slightly different standpoint, incentives to encourage greater inclusion of people who actually need the financial and educational opportunity made available by the act.

Written into almost every governmental, institutional, corporate company policy, hiring manual, employee handbook, training, etc., we will find that this same "social experiment" is under way, a response to another social experiment in which discrimination, segregation and an absence of civil rights and equal opportunities were the status quo.

The article provides other "evidence" that seems to indicate that the author believes the GIVE Act to be some sort of thinly disguised socialist/fascist effort to pick the pockets of the American public in an effort to force young people to volunteer for government-mandated charity work. (Geist and I agree on this at least: Forced volunteerism is a contradiction in terms.) By midway through the article, a slightly different agenda becomes evident; a slippery slope of antiliberal, anti-Democratic hyperbole casts some doubt on the more rational arguments.

President [Barack] Obama is referenced, unfavorably, in a completely unrelated policy regarding tax laws (and caps on deductible charitable contributions). Shortly thereafter, there is some JFK [John F. Kennedy] and Andrew Johnson bashing, and while I admire the historical reference, I fail to see what our 17th president (yes, I had to look it up) has to do with proving that a bill (providing more opportunity for service learning, job training and educational funding) is such a bad idea.

Money Well Spent

The article continues to state that the AmeriCorps program is, first: ". . . a waste of money," and a few paragraphs later (quoting conservative author James Bovard) nothing more

A Lot of Work to Do

I've met hundreds of AmeriCorps members through Habitat [for Humanity]. Of the members I actually served with, more than half are currently serving with other nonprofits or in a public service capacity. Every person I served with continues to volunteer. Service sticks. My team members are proof of that.

The message I want to leave you with is that AmeriCorps members are working to make our country greater. We're proud of our work to improve our country and our communities. . . . We have a lot of work to do.

Thomas Daigle, Testimony Before the House Committee on Education and Labor, Subcommittee on Healthy Families and Communities, February 27, 2007.

than ". . . a paid internship." I was surprised to hear that AmeriCorps is a waste of money, and I imagine that the thousands of people who benefit from it each year will be, too. Furthermore, I'm at a loss as to why a paid internship is a bad thing, even when the government is footing the bill.

After all, it seems like money well spent. I consider the engagement of underemployed people into service dedicated to providing disaster preparedness, health care, childhood development, environmental quality, energy efficiency, crime reduction and civic commitment—in exchange providing those people with work experience, educational opportunity and personal accountability to their community—to be a pretty good deal.

This is especially true given that the cost of this bill runs each taxpayer about $3 per person, per year—according to www.govtrack.us, a nonpartisan civic group that keeps tabs on Congress.

The final straw for me, in terms of finding the article to be an unreasonable attack on the GIVE Act, is the claim that people trained to work within the public sector (for example, those engaging in government-funded service learning programs) will be unable to work in the private sector afterward.

Huh?

Not a Fair-Minded Assessment

It's important to remember that these are opinion pieces. Whether it's Geist's opinion, my opinion or any other op-ed writer's opinion, we should always be informed well enough to back up our opinions. We're not just presenting facts and we're not reporting news in a purely objective fashion. There's no such thing as an objective opinion any more than there can be a forced volunteer.

Without the apparent predisposition to condemn all that is Democrat, I'd have been much more likely to seriously consider arguments against House Bill 1388. (After plowing through it, I agree with most—not all—of the ideas introduced in this legislation.)

The *Vanguard* article "GIVE back" provides no fair-minded assessment or even a minor consideration of possible advantages of the GIVE Act; instead it links irrelevant and anecdotal facts to the issue, "proof" that the liberal agenda will lead us all straight into poverty. In the end, this just comes off like partisan bias, maybe even a little bit like a conspiracy theory.

> "AmeriCorps members gain new and
> useful skills, advance their education,
> and become more connected to their
> communities."

AmeriCorps Improves Lives and Strengthens Communities

LaMonica Shelton, Brooke Nicholas, Lillian Dote, and Robert Grimm

In the following viewpoint, LaMonica Shelton, Brooke Nicholas, Lillian Dote, and Robert Grimm maintain that AmeriCorps members gain useful career skills, connect to their communities, and further their education. AmeriCorps alumni report that they learn leadership, communication, and teamwork skills that they later use at work, the authors claim. Moreover, they assert, 41 percent of members went on to obtain a bachelor's degree. In addition to providing immediate benefits, AmeriCorps helps communities develop the infrastructure needed to meet pressing needs. Shelton, Nicholas, and Dote are policy analysts and Grimm is director and special counsel to the chief executive officer of the Corporation for National and Community Service, Office of Research and Policy Development.

LaMonica Shelton, Brooke Nicholas, Lillian Dote, and Robert Grimm, "AmeriCorps: Changing Lives, Changing America," Corporation for National and Community Service, 2007.

As you read, consider the following questions:

1. According to Shelton, Nicholas, Dote, and Grimm, how many community volunteers did AmeriCorps members recruit, train, and manage in 2006?

2. What do the authors claim is the only goal that Ameri-Corps members rank higher than gaining new skills?

3. Why do the authors assert that AmeriCorps members with less education and experience engaging in their community gain more benefits from membership?

AmeriCorps operates under the auspices of the Corporation for National and Community Service [the Corporation], an independent federal agency. AmeriCorps is a network of three programs—Volunteers in Service to America [VISTA], National Civilian Community Corps (NCCC), and AmeriCorps State and National (State/National)—that each year supports 75,000 Americans in service to meet critical needs in education, the environment, public safety, disaster relief, and other areas. Since 1994, 500,000 AmeriCorps members have provided more than 630 million hours of service with tens of thousands of nonprofit organizations, public agencies, and faith-based organizations nationwide. Members tutor and mentor youth, build affordable housing, run after-school programs, care for the elderly, clean parks and streams, and respond to disasters. They also recruit, train, and manage community volunteers—more than 1.4 million in 2006 alone. In return for their service, AmeriCorps members receive a Segal AmeriCorps Education Award that they can use to pay for college or pay back qualified student loans. Members have earned more than $1.2 billion in education awards since 1994.

The Corporation's mission is to improve lives, strengthen communities, and foster civic engagement through service and volunteering. As each member takes the AmeriCorps pledge, he or she commits "to make our people safer, smarter, and healthier" by providing services that support the Corporation's mission. Members also pledge to uphold this commitment even after their year of service, a promise that is taken very seriously by our former members (alumni), as evidenced by their continued volunteering and civic participation.

While previous research has focused on the impact of AmeriCorps programs on communities, this report [from which this viewpoint was taken] looks at the impact that AmeriCorps has on the members who serve and the organizations that sponsor them. Based on data collected by the Corporation from 1999 to 2006 through the "AmeriCorps Longitudinal Study" and three satisfaction surveys, this report demonstrates that AmeriCorps members gain new and useful skills, advance their education, and become more connected to their communities. True to their pledge, AmeriCorps members continue to volunteer in their communities after their term of service ends, and are more likely to enter public service careers than a comparable group of individuals who did not serve with AmeriCorps. The report also shows that the organizations where AmeriCorps members serve highly value them because they help the organizations to expand their reach and effectiveness toward achieving their missions.

The Impact on AmeriCorps Members

AmeriCorps members are highly satisfied with their service experience. Many attribute much of that satisfaction to the invaluable experience gained from their service, including the opportunity to acquire additional skills for school and work. Alumni overwhelmingly report that AmeriCorps has positively affected their lives. As a result of their service, they enhanced their skills and strengthened their desire to continue volunteering.

In looking more closely at members' satisfaction levels, we find:

- 91 percent of members report that their overall Ameri-Corps service experience was excellent or good.

- 94 percent would re-enroll in AmeriCorps if given the opportunity.

- 95 percent would recommend AmeriCorps to a friend or family member.

Skill Development

Through the "AmeriCorps Member Satisfaction Survey," we find that members join AmeriCorps for a number of reasons. Forty-six percent of members join AmeriCorps to gain new skills as their primary or secondary reason (27 percent and 19 percent, respectively). Helping communities is the only goal that ranks higher (52 percent). AmeriCorps helped many members develop new skills. Almost all (99 percent) report their primary or secondary goal to acquire new skills was met.

Furthermore, 90 percent of members report that they have gained new skills from their AmeriCorps experience, regardless of whether it was their primary or secondary goal for joining. These skills prove to be useful, to members in their education and career pursuits, as 91 percent of alumni report that they have used the skills gained from their AmeriCorps service.

According to the "AmeriCorps Alumni Survey," members report acquiring skills such as leadership, teamwork, communication, time management, and decision making. When analyzing long-term effects from the "AmeriCorps Longitudinal Study," we see members experience a greater gain in basic work skills when compared to a similar group of individuals who have no AmeriCorps experience.

An Ethic of Service and Civic Engagement

Although members tend to already be a highly civically engaged group, our findings show that most continue to be actively engaged in their community after their service with

AmeriCorps. According to the "AmeriCorps Current Member Survey," 80 percent say they are likely to participate in community service as a result of their AmeriCorps experience.

Results from the "AmeriCorps Alumni Survey" reveal that close to that same number did volunteer after AmeriCorps—72 percent of members report that they have volunteered since completing their service. What's more, alumni contribute a considerable amount of time to volunteering after AmeriCorps. In fact, over half (57 percent) volunteer more than 80 hours total two to three years after completing their AmeriCorps service.

Further evidence of AmeriCorps's influence on members is demonstrated through the "AmeriCorps Longitudinal Study" by comparing the habits of members after service with a group of individuals who chose not to enroll in AmeriCorps. We surveyed members who served in AmeriCorps between 1999 and 2000 about their volunteer activities in their communities since completing their terms with AmeriCorps (between fall 2000 and fall 2002).

We find members who did not volunteer prior to AmeriCorps are more likely than the comparison group to volunteer after their service (a 25-percentage-point difference). What this tells us is that service through AmeriCorps sparks an interest in many members to become engaged in their communities after their program experience.

A Pipeline to Public Service

AmeriCorps alumni are significantly more likely than a comparable group of non-AmeriCorps members to enter into a public service career such as teaching, public safety, social work, and military service. According to the "AmeriCorps Alumni Survey," 35 percent of members report working in the public sector and 31 percent in the nonprofit sector since completing service. In fact, many members go on to pursue careers with people in need, including 67 percent of employed alumni who work with high-poverty populations and 33 percent who work with the elderly. Members who reported that they had been employed since completing their term of service with AmeriCorps were asked a series of follow-up questions, including questions about the population(s) with which they worked. When we look at the "AmeriCorps Longitudinal Study" to determine the long-term impacts of AmeriCorps, we find members more likely to be employed in public service than those from the comparison group—a seven-percentage-point difference.

The Connection to Education

Many members join AmeriCorps to gain experiences that will help them decide what kind of work they would like to do in the future. Some join in order to gain practical, hands-on experience that will help them in their future career. Others join to determine what their next step in life will be. Results from the "AmeriCorps Member Satisfaction Survey" show that 71 percent report the Segal AmeriCorps Education Award was another incentive for them joining AmeriCorps. Members often report that as a result of their AmeriCorps service experience they are more likely to continue with their education. Moreover, three years after enrolling in AmeriCorps, 41 percent of members report they obtained a bachelor's degree.

Furthermore, the "AmeriCorps Member Satisfaction Survey" revealed that members with a four-year degree are more likely to have volunteered before AmeriCorps than members without a four-year college degree. Of these two groups, those without a degree (who did not previously volunteer) are twice as likely to become volunteers after their AmeriCorps experience. Among members with some or no college experience, 22 percent had not volunteered before joining AmeriCorps. Through the "AmeriCorps Alumni Survey" we find that of this 22 percent, a little more than half (52 percent) report volunteering since completing service in AmeriCorps. Members with a four-year degree who did not volunteer before Ameri-Corps also increase their civic engagement. Thirteen percent of members with college degrees had not volunteered before joining AmeriCorps. Of this 13 percent, more than a third (36 percent) report volunteering since completing service in Ame-riCorps.

These education differences speak to the possibility that while all types of members receive positive benefits from their AmeriCorps service, members with less than a college educa-tion and with less experience engaging in their community gain slightly more benefits than others.

The Impact on Organizations

AmeriCorps members serve through thousands of different national and local organizations, helping them expand their reach, serve more people, and better achieve their mission. These groups include community and faith-based organiza-tions, institutions of higher education, schools, public agen-cies, Native American tribes, and more. AmeriCorps was de-signed to ensure that funding and decision making occurs with those who know their states and communities best.

By providing existing organizations with dedicated indi-viduals who make an intensive service commitment, Ameri-Corps helps organizations accomplish more—both through the members who provide direct and capacity-building ser-vices and through the additional community volunteers whom they recruit and supervise. This section looks at the positive effects AmeriCorps members have on the nonprofit organiza-tions they serve.

The local nonprofit and community organizations that have AmeriCorps members have extremely favorable views about AmeriCorps. They report that members greatly contrib-ute to their efforts to build the capacity necessary to do even greater work in their communities. The "AmeriCorps Member Satisfaction Survey" shows that 93 percent of organizations rate the members who served with them as excellent or good, and 93 percent report that members help them to serve additional persons in the community.

Volunteer Recruitment and Management

Beyond their direct service, AmeriCorps members play a key role in helping organizations increase their capacity by recruiting more volunteers and serving as volunteer coordinators who train, manage, and support volunteers. Last year alone, AmeriCorps members recruited or managed more than 1.4 million volunteers.

Volunteers are arguably an organization's most important resource. They are vital for helping an organization expand its reach in a community. The Corporation's "Volunteer Management Capacity Study" demonstrated the importance of implementing effective volunteer management practices (such as training and screening volunteers) as necessary ingredients to successfully recruit and manage volunteers. That study found that one of the most popular capacity-building options among charities with social service outreach activities is placing someone like an AmeriCorps member with the organization and making that member responsible for volunteer recruitment and management.

As we learned from the "Volunteer Management Capacity Study," an estimated four out of every five public charities rely upon volunteers. AmeriCorps recognizes the value of volunteers and many programs assign members to recruit and manage volunteers. Eighty-four percent of organizations in the study report that members helped the organization to leverage additional volunteers. In fact, the "AmeriCorps Member Satisfaction Survey" shows us that most members spend at least some time recruiting and/or managing volunteers (76 percent recruit and 62.5 percent manage volunteers). We believe the presence of the members and their efforts to increase the number of managed volunteers within an organization relates to the percentage of organizations who report that members have helped the nonprofit to serve additional persons in the community (93 percent).

Evidence of Additional Capacity-Building Efforts

Nonprofits further report that members help them develop additional partnerships and increase their in-kind donations. One way for an organization to expand its reach is to develop more partnerships. Partnerships can broaden an organization's expertise, strengthen resources, and provide an entry into new communities. Many successful service projects and programs are built on partnerships similar to the Habitat for Humanity example, which is just one of many partnership examples. Resources from AmeriCorps, including members, play a key role; in fact, 88 percent of organizations report that AmeriCorps has helped them to develop partnerships with other organizations, according to the "AmeriCorps Organization Survey."

In helping to build capacity, organizations also look to increase the amount of in-kind and other resources they receive to help expand their reach in communities. Members help coordinate the collection of food, clothing, and other items, as well as help to target and augment development efforts. In addition to raising funds and writing grants, members are helping to bring in donations of goods or services to organizations, as 62 percent of organizations report.

Helping Communities

Overall, our findings suggest that the AmeriCorps service experience reaps multiple benefits for members, which contribute to their high satisfaction levels. AmeriCorps provides opportunities for members to develop a variety of new and useful skills they can apply in their future endeavors, and most members report that they have indeed applied these skills.

AmeriCorps members also say that their experience has contributed to their interest in advancing their education. A majority of members report that the Segal AmeriCorps Education Award is an incentive for them to join the program, and many who did not have a four-year degree at the time they served go on to obtain one later.

Although most members continue to volunteer after their service, we find that AmeriCorps sparks future community engagement among people who do not have a history of service, demonstrating AmeriCorps's benefits to them years afterward.

Members simultaneously provide numerous benefits to communities. As they assist organizations in increasing their capacity to manage more volunteers and serve additional people, members are also helping organizations develop the infrastructure necessary to meet the needs of their communities after the members have left the organization.

> *"Those who cherish the independence of American philanthropy and the nonprofits it supports actually have reason for worry."*

AmeriCorps's Expansion Threatens American Philanthropy

Howard Husock

Federal grant programs such as AmeriCorps threaten creative charity efforts often fashioned in response to ineffective government social service programs, argues Howard Husock in the following viewpoint. Large grant programs are tempting for independent organizations with limited funds, he maintains. Unfortunately, to get federal money, social entrepreneurs must meet federal directives on what needs doing, even if the organization believes these directives are counterproductive, Husock contends. Forcing innovative charities to operate on government-approved projects to receive federal funds is not the best way to help American communities, he reasons. Husock, vice president for policy research at the Manhattan Institute, heads its Social Entrepreneurship Initiative.

As you read, consider the following questions:

1. According to the founder of Upwardly Global, to what type of work did the government steer skilled immigrants?

2. Why does Husock claim that AmeriCorps is nothing like the Roosevelt-era Works Progress Administration or the Civilian Conservation Corps?

3. According to the legislation, with whom must nonprofits on the receiving end of federal funds consult?

This week [April 2009], the president [Barack Obama] signed into law the Edward M. Kennedy Serve America Act, which authorizes a huge expansion of the AmeriCorps program, potentially tripling the number of its government-paid "volunteers." The legislation—which also promises federal funds for "effective solutions developed by social entrepreneurs"—was heralded as a victory for patriotism and public service. It was enough to draw Jimmy Carter to share the podium with Ted Kennedy—both on hand for the signing ceremony at a charter school in a poor section of Washington, D.C. But is it truly good news? Those who cherish the independence of American philanthropy and the nonprofits it supports actually have reason for worry.

Responding to Ineffective Government Programs

The past two decades have seen an explosion of new, inventive nonprofits established and operated with little or no government support. They stand in notable contrast to established, large organizations—from Catholic Charities to the Salvation Army—which, in many cases, have come to rely on government contracts. The new wave seemed different. Many of the "social entrepreneurs" to which the new national service bill refers were themselves frustrated with ineffective government social-service programs.

"Volunteers." Cartoon by Ed Fischer. www.CartoonStock.com.

The founder of Upwardly Global, an immigrant-assistance program based in San Francisco, had seen government programs steering skilled immigrants to menial jobs and worked instead to find positions that would make use of their qualifications. The founders of the Boston-based Year Up sought to replace outdated government job-training programs with technical education and corporate apprenticeships for urban young adults. The founders of such nonprofits have been disciplined by the challenge of finding funds—mixing philanthropic support with fees from businesses and clients—and learning that a good cause is not enough; results matter. Some in this new wave of social entrepreneurs even took personal risks. The founders of the SEED Charter School, for example, where the president signed the bill, took out personal loans and went without salaries in order to fund the renovation of the school's building.

A Threat to Creative Independent Efforts

But the Kennedy Act threatens to thwart this creative movement. It will throw so much money at nascent [new] programs that these otherwise independent efforts will lurch after federal dollars and bend toward government directives.

Take the AmeriCorps expansion. Its name notwithstanding, the program is nothing like the Roosevelt-era Works Progress Administration or the Civilian Conservation Corps—government-run operations with recruits in uniform, building trails and bridges. AmeriCorps is a grant program in which *people* are the prize. Organizations that want its federally subsidized free labor must apply to "service commissions" established, by statute, in all 50 states and whose members are appointed by governors. Inevitably, these commissions risk choosing winners and losers based on politics, not just merit.

Then there's the legislation's new "social innovation fund," which promises to bring with it big money: five-year grants, renewable for another five, of between $1 million and $10 million. The funds will come, however, with tight strings—government will specify what most needs doing. Organizations must be "focused on improving measurable outcomes in such matters as education for economically disadvantaged students, child and youth development, reductions in poverty or increases in economic opportunity."

In language reminiscent of the War on Poverty's infamous "maximum feasible participation" requirement for community input, nonprofits on the receiving end of the fund's dollars will have to "consult with a diverse cross-section of community representatives." In short, the legislative language seeks to codify the goals of those, like California Rep. Xavier Becerra, who have been telling the nonprofit world to focus its work on low-income and minority communities in approved ways—or risk losing their tax deductibility.

Sadly, social entrepreneurs—who have often started organizations to help us cope with the failure of government programs—may well be tempted by the big money. But that won't be the best way to serve America.

| "Every able-bodied person who receives unemployment compensation should be required to volunteer part-time for AmeriCorps."

AmeriCorps Can Put the Unemployed to Work

Lanny Davis

In the following viewpoint, Lanny Davis maintains that while seeking work, unemployed Americans can earn some money while serving as AmeriCorps volunteers. Money being paid for unemployment compensation and to support the AmeriCorps program could fund the initiative, he claims. In addition, Davis asserts, this solution could take advantage of a bureaucracy already in place. Moreover, like Franklin D. Roosevelt's work programs during the 1930s, such a plan would immediately put people to work and help communities at the same time. Davis, former special counsel to President Bill Clinton, served as a member of President George W. Bush's Privacy and Civil Liberties Oversight Board.

Lanny Davis, "Putting the Unemployed to Work for AmeriCorps—and How to Pay for It," *The Hill*, October 21, 2009. Reproduced by permission.

As you read, consider the following questions:

1. Why is the unemployment situation far worse when broken down into segments of the American population, in Davis's opinion?

2. Why does the author believe being required to work for AmeriCorps to receive unemployment benefits is fair?

3. How does the author answer conservatives who object to any increase in taxes?

The national unemployment figure announced as of the end of September [2009] is bleak and distressing: 9.8 percent. Since the start of the recession in December 2007, the number of unemployed has more than doubled—an increase of 7.6 million, to 15.1 million people. If you take into account those who are unemployed but have stopped looking for jobs, the number is probably over 17 million.

But the situation is far worse when you break it down into segments of the population. African-American unemployment is at least 15.4 percent—more than 60 percent higher than among white males.

A Need for New Ideas

So what to do? The president's stimulus package may have resulted in the unemployment figure being lower than would otherwise be the case.

That's a difficult case to prove. But we need some new ideas to create new jobs—immediately. The human tragedies of pervasive unemployment throughout our country cannot wait the one to two years some say it will take before the stimulus programs fully kick in and start creating millions of new jobs.

So here's my idea: Every able-bodied person who receives unemployment compensation should be required to volunteer part-time for AmeriCorps, the American public service program begun by President Bill Clinton in 1993. (In April 2009, President Barack Obama signed legislation tripling the appropriation for AmeriCorps to its current total of $5.7 billion over eight years.) I say part-time because they need at least one day a week to go job hunting, a requirement in order to continue to receive unemployment benefits. I propose this be a requirement because it's only fair for recipients of unemployment payments to give back to the community. Moreover, for most it will be a positive experience—getting them out of the house and increasing feelings of self-worth.

By using AmeriCorps as the structure to absorb these new workers and put them to work immediately, no new bureaucracy need be created. And we know these are not "make-work" jobs but real contributions to the public good, as Ameri-Corps has proven over the years.

For example, right now, AmeriCorps workers are mentoring and tutoring children living in poverty, caring for the elderly, cleaning up neighborhoods and national forests, repairing old houses, working in hospitals and emergency rooms, teaching computer skills, cleaning up streets in inner-city neighborhoods, working in national parks on conservation and other environmental projects, and supplementing skilled workers on current roads, bridges and public-utilities construction and rehabilitation projects.

This is not meant to be a permanent public works program. It is meant to be temporary, until the private sector rebounds from the near-total disaster of last year's meltdown.

Possible Sources of Financing

How to finance? I don't know the exact cost required—I'll leave the Congressional Budget Office or other budget experts to figure that out—but I'll take a stab at three possible sources of financing.

First, use at least some of the funds already being paid for unemployment compensation (financed by an eight-tenths-of-

1-percent payment by employers to the IRS [Internal Revenue Service], and administered by the states).

Second, add new money diverted from the currently funded stimulus program—again, specifically paid to Ameri-Corps and required to be used to hire new people from the ranks of the unemployed.

Third, if necessary, add a temporary, special surtax—for example, 1 percent for those earning more than $100,000 a year, 2 percent between $250,000 and $500,000 and 3 percent above $500,000. This would result, roughly at an average marginal rate of 40 percent, of a per-person incremental cost of $400, $800 and $1,200 per person per year, respectively. The surtax would be "sunsetted" and would therefore need to be renewed each year. As unemployment drops, the surtax would be phased out entirely, say at 5 percent or lower.

But, again, this will be a new kind of tax—let's call it a targeted tax—with proceeds only allowed to go directly into a trust account, with AmeriCorps as trustee, to be used only to create brand-new AmeriCorps jobs from the ranks of the un-employed—in short, not allowed under the law to be diverted to pay for $1,000 toilet seats or bridges to nowhere.

Getting People Working

OK, good readers of this column: That's my idea. I am sure there are plenty of ways to poke holes in it, especially for some conservatives who object to any increase in taxes, pe-riod. But my arguments to them: The amounts are small rela-tive to income, it is sunsetted annually, it is targeted and pro-ceeds cannot be diverted for pork [government resources used by politicians to gain favor].

But one thing I know about this idea: If enacted, it will immediately or nearly immediately get people working and doing good at the same time, much as occurred when FDR [President Franklin D. Roosevelt] between 1933 and '35 cre-ated the WPA [Works Progress Administration], the CCC [Civilian Conservation Corps] and other emergency job "relief" programs. Except FDR didn't have the benefit of an existing and much-praised organization already in place such as AmeriCorps.

Anyone have a better idea for immediate job creation for the public good without increasing the deficit?

> "AmeriCorps jobs, with annual stipends
> of around $10,000 or $11,000, are not
> the equivalent of good jobs."

Replacing Nonprofit Personnel with AmeriCorps Volunteers Reduces the Value of Nonprofit Work

Rick Cohen

In the following viewpoint, Rick Cohen asserts that using low-paid AmeriCorps volunteers to replace nonprofit workers sends the wrong message about the value of nonprofit work. Paying less than a living wage suggests that nonprofit jobs are poverty-wage jobs in which caring and concern take the place of technical and professional skill, he maintains. This perception does not help build an effective nonprofit workforce, Cohen claims. Moreover, he reasons, substituting low-paid volunteers for nonprofit human service jobs creates an industry standard that such work needs little compensation. Cohen, a correspondent for the Nonprofit Quarterly, *was executive director of the National Committee for Responsive Philanthropy.*

Rick Cohen, "Nonprofit Jobs Need Better Pay," *Nonprofit Quarterly*, February 26, 2009. Reproduced by permission.

As you read, consider the following questions:

1. Why does Cohen claim that 2009, the time he wrote the following viewpoint, was a difficult time to challenge inadequate nonprofit wages?

2. What did a nation—now prepared to accept nearly anything that will generate paychecks—not long ago decry, in the author's opinion?

3. In the author's view, why is it a terrible message to send to the human services delivery part of the nonprofit sector that nonprofit jobs are low paying?

The current wave of enthusiasm for service and volunteerism in the nonprofit sector—key components of the Obama-Biden campaign platform that are likely to come to pass with the enactment of the [Edward M. Kennedy] Serve America Act [which was signed into law on April 21, 2009] co-sponsored by Senators Orrin Hatch and Ted Kennedy—risks distorting the American public's perception of what constitutes good nonprofit jobs, particularly in human services.

This is a difficult time to challenge inadequate nonprofit wages.

Unemployment and underemployment have skyrocketed. According to the Bureau of Labor Statistics, 4.1 million people became unemployed in the last 12 months, including nearly 600,000 in January 2009 alone.

People counted as "involuntarily part-time" because they can't find good full-time jobs increased by 3.1 million over the year.

Facing the worst recession since the 1930s, a nation that not long ago decried Wal-Mart and Target jobs as abysmal and called for government contractors to pay "living wages" now seems prepared to accept nearly anything that will generate paychecks.

The economic stimulus package signed by President [Barack] Obama aims at stimulating construction in "shovel-ready" public improvement projects and jump-starting demand for cars and trucks that will reemploy laid-off Detroit autoworkers.

Even with wage concessions, construction and manufacturing jobs won't be sub-living wage.

A Conflicting Message

But what is the message for nonprofit human service jobs in this economic crisis?

The major initiatives in the public's consciousness to build and sustain employment in the nonprofit sector generally sound like pretty low-wage, volunteer responses to the need to fill nonprofit line jobs with decently paid and trained professionals.

During the presidential campaign, candidates Obama and [Joe] Biden released a document titled, "Helping All Americans Serve Their Country," heavily oriented to a range of stipended and volunteer additions to the AmeriCorps family of programs.

For example, the statement called for an increase in the size of AmeriCorps from its current roughly 75,000 slots to 250,000 through initiatives focused on classroom teaching, health services, clean energy and homeland security.

This is just about exactly the projected AmeriCorps size in the Kennedy-Hatch bill.

AmeriCorps is a program that many Americans adore for a variety of reasons ranging from its impact on participants' civic participation to the notion of doing community service work to earn money to be used for college or graduate school tuition.

Not Good Wages

But AmeriCorps jobs, with annual stipends of around $10,000 or $11,000, are not the equivalent of good jobs.

They are generally below living wage, barely above the upcoming July 2009 federal minimum wage of $7.25 an hour.

Realize further than more than half of AmeriCorps participants are actually only part-time, probably working their tails off, like most AmeriCorps people, nonetheless.

Just read the AmeriCorps jobs tips for helping participants find affordable-housing accommodations on these living stipends.

AmeriCorps stipends do not constitute good wages in the nonprofit human services sector.

But as nonprofits are being compelled due to philanthropic and government cutbacks to lay off staff, replacing them with AmeriCorps bodies could lead to the deleterious idea that nonprofits don't need to pay well, pay living wages, offer benefits, offer union-like job protections, offer full-time jobs, create long-term career paths, or recruit and build professional skills among their staff in order to deliver their goods and services.

A batch of observers has suggested that these 250,000 AmeriCorps slots be counted as stimulus-induced and stimulus-inducing job creation.

The public impression that nonprofit jobs are low-paid, poverty-wage jobs in which enthusiasm and caring take the place of technical skills and professional continuity is not the way to build and sustain a nonprofit workforce.

Moreover, it is a terrible message to send for the human services delivery part of the nonprofit sector in which people of color and women constitute disproportionately high percentages of the workforce.

The "Casualization of Jobs"

The downside risk of substituting low-paid stipended volunteers for nonprofit human services jobs is the dynamic of the "casualization of jobs" that Robert Kuttner of the *American Prospect* describes as jobs that pay low wages [and] offer weak or no benefits and little in the way of job protections, which he describes as the "industry standard" in the human service sector. He suggests an alternative to the drift toward casual jobs as the norm in the human services sector, nonprofit and for-profit:

"Since most human service costs are paid socially, choices about how to compensate workers are social decisions. . . Congress could require that any job in the human services supported in whole or in part by federal funds would have to pay a professional wage and be part of a career track [and a] minimum starting annual salary might be $24,000 a year, or about $12 an hour . . ."

That's not much of a salary, but it might stanch the public's thinking that the nonprofit workforce can be sustained with an oversupply of caring and concern to make up for the shortfalls in take-home pay and job protections.

Despite the campaign's overreliance on volunteerism as the labor solution for the nonprofit sector . . . there is an audience in the new administration for remembering the importance of good jobs in the nonprofit sector.

An important hint came from Shirley Sagawa, rumored to be in line for a top Obama administration post, who suggested it might be more important to focus on the quality of AmeriCorps jobs, not simply by the "number of bodies" in the program.

One national nonprofit leader recently called on Congress to "ensure that nonprofit workers stay on the job" if the nonprofit sector is going to be able to fulfill its role in the national economic recovery.

That is not going to happen if the national recovery classifies private sector jobs as worthy of decent wages and protections, but nonprofit jobs to be filled by people paid little or nothing.

Periodical Bibliography

The following articles have been selected to supplement the diverse views presented in this chapter.

Rick Boucher	"Capitol Commentary: Consider AmeriCorps," *New River Voice* (Virginia), September 1, 2009.
Edward Cline	"Obama's 'Blood Tax': Compulsory 'National Service' Revisited," *Capitalism*, May 18, 2009.
Examiner (Washington, DC)	"Expanded AmeriCorps Has an Authoritarian Feel," March 26, 2009.
Vincent Gioia	"The 'GIVE ACT' Should Be Called the 'TAKE ACT,'" *Right Side News*, April 13, 2009. www.rightsidenews.com.
Bethany Godsoe	"What Obama's Call to National Service Needs," *Christian Science Monitor*, May 20, 2009.
Gene Healy	"Serve America Lets Congress Take Another Bow," *DC Examiner*, April 7, 2009.
Stratton Lawrence	"Americut?" *Charleston City Paper* (South Carolina), March 29, 2006.
Shirley Sagawa	"How Quickly Can National Service Grow?" Center for American Progress, February 2010. www.americanprogress.org.
Andrea Stone	"White House Hopes Volunteer Initiative Will Help Economy," *USA Today*, June 19, 2009.
Washington Times	"Rotten to the AmeriCorps," February 10, 2010.

For Further Discussion

Chapter 1

1. Of the four visions of national service explored by Peter Frumkin and Brendan Miller, which, if any, do you think is most necessary to promote? What evidence in the viewpoint led you to this conclusion? Explain.

2. Although Sheldon Richman agrees with Peter Frumkin and Brendan Miller that doing good deeds is a valued American trait, he feels that government-sponsored national service is inappropriate in a free society. He believes that Americans should serve by choice, not by mandate or through taxes that support government national service programs. What examples do the authors of these opposing views cite to support their points of view? Which examples do you find persuasive? Citing examples from the viewpoints, explain your answer.

3. David L. Caprara cites the success of several programs to support his claim that national service solves social problems. James Bovard cites evidence that national service programs have not adequately proven they have any social impact. Can both positions be true? Does the type of evidence these authors cite influence your answer? Which position do you find more persuasive? Explain.

Chapter 2

1. In his speech, George W. Bush recognizes the national service of numerous volunteers. James Bovard maintains that national service has little impact and is used by politicians to put them in a good light. Does Bovard's claim change the way in which you interpret Bush's speech, or

are the volunteer efforts that Bush recognizes enough to convince you that national service helps communities? Explain.

2. Sara Falconer argues that some national service programs have the effect of doing more harm than good and that those who create some of these programs have ulterior motives. Do you think the political activist volunteerism she recommends will address her concerns? Do you think her concerns, if true, should discourage volunteer relief efforts? Do any of the other viewpoints in this chapter inform your answers?

3. Paul Thornton argues that national service programs unfairly target the young. Do you agree? Explain.

4. Examine the source information for the viewpoints in this chapter. How do the audiences for these publications differ? Do you think the authors' rhetoric changes as a result? Does this influence whether you think some viewpoints are more persuasive than others? Explain.

Chapter 3

1. Michael G. Hypes claims that service learning teaches civic responsibility. John B. Egger believes that service is unnecessary to teach students to be better citizens. Both authors are professors but appear to have different views on the role of education. How do their beliefs about the role of education influence their views? Which do you find more persuasive?

2. What rhetorical strategies do the editors of *Practical Homeschooling* use to assert their claim that service learning is inappropriate in a free society? Do you find this strategy persuasive? Explain why or why not.

Chapter 4

1. Shirley Sagawa advocates government support of national service because of the positive impact it has in American communities. Patrick Krey believes that because government-supported national service is not voluntary, it is un-American. Since the ideals expressed by the authors conflict, how do you as the reader determine which viewpoint you find more persuasive? What evidence provided by either author might change your views? Explain.

2. Michelle Malkin claims that national service programs are designed to promote a radical social agenda. Fiona Bruce disputes this claim. Bruce claims that giving volunteers a living wage is a good use of American tax dollars. How does each author's view of the role of government differ? How does this view inform each author's rhetoric? Which do you find more persuasive? Explain.

3. LaMonica Shelton, Brooke Nicholas, Lillian Dote, and Robert Grimm claim that the benefits to both volunteers and the communities they serve warrant continued support of AmeriCorps. Howard Husock argues that AmeriCorps threatens charity organizations that operate more effectively than government programs. What examples do the authors cite to support their points of view? Which examples do you find persuasive? Explain.

4. Lanny Davis argues that putting the unemployed to work with AmeriCorps jobs is an effective way to help the unemployed and support the economy. Rick Cohen opposes AmeriCorps jobs because the low wages offered diminish the value of nonprofit work. Which argument do you find more persuasive? Explain.

Organizations to Contact

The editors have compiled the following list of organizations concerned with the issues debated in this book. The descriptions are derived from materials provided by the organizations. All have publications or information available for interested readers. The list was compiled on the date of publication of the present volume; the information provided here may change. Be aware that many organizations take several weeks or longer to respond to inquiries, so allow as much time as possible.

American Enterprise Institute (AEI)
1150 Seventeenth Street NW, Washington, DC   20036
(202) 862-5800 • fax: (202) 862-7177
website: www.aei.org

The American Enterprise Institute (AEI) is a research institute dedicated to preserving limited government, private enterprise, and a strong foreign policy and national defense. The institute publishes the magazine the *American*, the current issue of which is available on its website. Also on its website, AEI publishes testimony, commentary, speeches, and aticles including "Attitudes About National Service" and "Is the US Public Service Academy a Good Idea?"

AmeriCorps
1201 New York Avenue NW, Washington, DC   20525
(202) 606-5000
e-mail: questions@americorps.gov
website: www.americorps.gov

AmeriCorps is a national service organization that offers seventy-five thousand opportunities each year for adults of all ages and backgrounds to serve through a network of partnerships with local and national nonprofit groups. The Edward M. Kennedy Serve America Act signed in April 2009 will expand this number to 250,000 by 2017. The AmeriCorps members address critical needs in communities all across America. On its website are fact sheets and personal stories and links to specific AmeriCorps programs such as VISTA, originally Volunteers in Service to America, and the National Community Civilian Corps (NCCC).

Brookings Institution

1775 Massachusetts Avenue NW, Washington, DC   20036
(202) 797-6000 • fax: (202) 797-6004
e-mail: brookinfo@brook.edu
website: www.brookings.edu

The Brookings Institution, founded in 1927, is a think tank that conducts research and education in foreign policy, economics, government, and the social sciences. Publications include the quarterly *Brookings Review*, periodic policy briefs, and books such as *United We Serve: National Service and the Future of Citizenship*.

Cato Institute

1000 Massachusetts Avenue NW
Washington, DC   20001-5403
(202) 842-0200 • fax: (202) 842-3490
e-mail: cato@cato.org
website: www.cato.org

The Cato Institute is a nonpartisan public policy research foundation dedicated to limiting the role of government and protecting individual liberties. It publishes the quarterly magazine *Regulation*, the bimonthly *Cato Policy Report*, and numerous policy papers and articles. Articles on national service include the report *National Service: The Enduring Panacea* and the blog commentary "You'll Get Served," both of which are available on its website.

Center for American Progress
1333 H Street NW, 10th Floor, Washington, DC   20005
(202) 682-1611 • fax: (202) 682-1867
website: www.americanprogress.org

The Center for American Progress was founded in 2003 to provide long-term leadership and support to the progressive movement, develop progressive policy ideas, critique the policy that stems from conservative values, and challenge the media to cover the issues that shape the national debate. It develops policies to address twenty-first-century challenges such as energy, national security, economic growth and opportunity, immigration, education, and health care. The center publishes the book *The American Way to Change: How National Service and Volunteers Are Transforming America.* It also publishes reports, many of which are available on its website, including *Students Can Improve National Service* and *How Quickly Can National Service Grow?*

Corporation for National and Community Service
1201 New York Avenue NW, Washington, DC   20525
(202) 606-5000
e-mail: info@cns.gov
website: www.nationalservice.gov

Borne from President George H.W. Bush's efforts to encourage volunteering and further developed by presidents Bill Clinton, George W. Bush, and Barack Obama, the Corporation for National and Community Service is a federal agency that engages more than 5 million Americans in service through Senior Corps, AmeriCorps, and Learn and Serve America. It also leads President Barack Obama's United We Serve, a nationwide service initiative created to help meet growing social needs resulting from the economic downturn. This initiative aims to both expand the impact of existing organizations by engaging new volunteers in their work and encourage volunteers to develop their own "do-it-yourself" projects. Serve.gov is the online resource for not only finding volunteer opportunities but also creating such opportunities.

Experience Corps
2120 L Street NW, Suite 610, Washington, DC   20037
(202) 478-6190 • fax: (202) 478-6162
e-mail: info@experiencecorps.org
website: www.experiencecorps.org

The Experience Corps is a volunteer organization in which Americans over age fifty-five tutor children in inner-city schools. The corps is based on the belief that through this generational exchange, children succeed, older adults thrive, and communities are made stronger. On its website the corps publishes news, research published in scholarly journals on the program's impact, and personal stories from Experience Corps members.

National Service-Learning Partnership
1825 Connecticut Avenue NW, Suite 800
Washington, DC   20009-5721
(202) 884-8356
www.service-learningpartnership.org

Founded in 2001 as part of the Academy for Educational Development, the National Service-Learning Partnership is dedicated to advancing service learning as a core part of every young person's education. The partnership website provides access to a national network of like-minded service-learning supporters, service-learning tools, resources, best practices, and opportunities to take action. It publishes the peer-reviewed *Information for Action: A Journal for Research on Service-Learning for Children and Youth*; the partnership's electronic monthly newsletter, *Service-Learning Advances*; and *Cathy's Corner*, an advice column on high-quality service-learning practice. Recent issues and archives of these publications are available on its website.

Peace Corps
1111 Twentieth Street NW, Washington, DC   20526
(800) 424-8580
website: www.peacecorps.gov

The Peace Corps traces its roots and mission to 1960, when then senator John F. Kennedy challenged students at the University of Michigan to serve their country in the cause of peace by living and working in developing countries. From that inspiration grew an agency of the federal government devoted to world peace and friendship. Since that time, nearly two hundred thousand Peace Corps Volunteers have served in 139 host countries to work on issues ranging from AIDS education to information technology and environmental preservation. The corps publishes the *Peace Corps Times*, a quarterly newsletter distributed to all Peace Corps volunteers in the field. The newsletter provides Peace Corps–related news from across the globe and allows volunteers to share information on their successful projects and endeavors with others in the Peace Corps community. Recent and past issues of the newsletter are available on the corps website.

Reason Foundation

3415 S. Sepulveda Boulevard, Suite 400
Los Angeles, CA   90034
(310) 391-2245 • fax: (310) 391-4395
website: www.reason.org

The Reason Foundation promotes individual freedoms and free-market principles and opposes US interventionism in foreign affairs. Its publications include the monthly *Reason* magazine, recent issues of which are available on its website. The foundation's website, linked to the Reason Public Policy Institute at www.rppi.org, publishes online versions of articles and reports, including "The Politics of Giving."

Youth Service America (YSA)

1101 Fifteenth Street NW, Suite 200, Washington, DC   20005
(202) 296-2992 • fax: (202) 296-4030
e-mail: info@ysa.org
website: www.ysa.org

Founded in 1986, Youth Service America (YSA) supports a global culture of engaged youth committed to a lifetime of service, learning leadership, and achievement. Its goal is to educate youth, teachers, community organizations, media, and public officials in the power of youth as problem solvers and to engage youth as volunteers, academic achievers, and community leaders. YSA works toward these goals through public campaigns such as Global Youth Service Day, by funding grants and awards geared to youth, and through training. YSA publishes news and fact sheets and its weekly e-newsletter for the service and service-learning fields, *National Service Briefing*. It also publishes a resource guide designed to engage youth in service-learning initiatives.

Bibliography of Books

AmeriCorps and National Civilian Community Corps
Pass the Fire: Stories About Service in America. Washington, DC: AmeriCorps/National Civilian Community Corps, 2003.

Janet S. Bixby and Judith L. Pace, eds.
Educating Democratic Citizens in Troubled Times. Albany: State University of New York Press, 2008.

William F. Buckley Jr.
Gratitude: Reflections on What We Owe to Our Country. New York: Random House, 1990.

Dan W. Butin
Service-Learning in Higher Education: Critical Issues and Directions. New York: Palgrave Macmillan, 2005.

Robert Coles
The Call of Service: A Witness to Idealism. Boston: Houghton Mifflin, 1993.

Corporation for National and Community Service
The Health Benefits of Volunteering: A Review of Recent Research. Washington, DC: Corporation for National and Community Service, Office of Research and Policy Development, 2007.

E.J. Dionne Jr., Kayla Meltzer Drogosz, and Robert E. Litan, eds.
United We Serve: National Service and the Future of Citizenship. Washington, DC: Brookings Institution Press, 2003.

Jon Duschinsky   *Philanthropy in a Flat World:*
                  Inspiration Through Globalization.
                  Hoboken, NJ: John Wiley & Sons,
                  2009.

Norton Garfinkle *Uniting America: Restoring the Vital*
and Daniel   *Center to American Democracy.* New
Yankelovich, eds. Haven, CT: Yale University Press,
                  2005.

Amanda Moore   *Civic Service Worldwide: Impacts and*
McBride and   *Inquiry.* Armonk, NY: M.E. Sharpe,
Michael   2007.
Sherraden, eds.

Lorraine McIlrath *Higher Education and Civic*
and Iain Mac   *Engagement: International*
Labhrainn, eds.   *Perspectives.* Burlington, VT: Ashgate,
                  2007.

Suzanne W.   *Renewing Civic Capacity: Preparing*
Morse   *College Students for Service and*
                  Citizenship. Washington, DC: School
                  of Education and Human
                  Development, George Washington
                  University, 1989.

Charles C.   *A Call to Civic Service: National*
Moskos   *Service for Country and Community.*
                  New York: Free Press, 1988.

Marvin Olasky   *The Tragedy of American Compassion.*
                  Washington, DC: Regnery Gateway,
                  1992.

S. Karthick Ramakrishnan and Irene Bloemraad, eds. — *Civic Hopes and Political Realities: Immigrants, Community Organization, and Political Engagement.* New York: Russell Sage Foundation, 2008.

Nancy C. Roberts, ed. — *The Age of Direct Citizen Participation.* Armonk, NY: M.E. Sharpe, 2008.

Shirley Sagawa — *The American Way to Change: How National Service and Volunteers Are Transforming America.* San Francisco: Jossey-Bass, 2010.

Michael J. Sandel — *Justice: What's the Right Thing to Do?* New York: Farrar, Straus and Giroux, 2009.

Kimberly Spring, Nathan Dietz, and Robert Grimm Jr. — *Education for Active Citizenship: Service-Learning, School-Based Service, and Youth Civic Engagement.* Washington, DC: Corporation for National and Community Service, 2006.

Sally Cahill Tannenbaum — *Research, Advocacy, and Political Engagement: Multidisciplinary Perspectives Through Service Learning.* Sterling, VA: Stylus, 2008.

Jonathan Tisch with Karl Weber — *Citizen You: Doing Your Part to Change the World.* New York: Crown, 2010.

Marie Watkins and Linda Braun — *Service-Learning: From Classroom to Community to Career.* Indianapolis, IN: JIST Life, 2005.

Index